Memories of The Royal Electrical Mechanical Engineers WWII

With Best Wishes
Sylvester Till

Memories of
The Royal Electrical
Mechanical Engineers
WWII

Personal Account
1939 to Demob August 1946

Sylvester Till

First published in 2007 by:
Stamford House Publishing

ISBN: 978-1-904985-51-8

Printed and bound in Great Britain by:
Stamford House Publishing
Remus House
Coltsfoot Drive
Woodston
Peterborough
PE7 9JX

Contents

Appendices

ACKNOWLEDGEMENT

I feel it must be recorded that I am very much indebted to Edna Calland, of Freckleton, for giving me lots of encouragement to write this book, for her great help in its typing and copying of all photographs, and for the many laughs along the way.

Thank you very much Edna.

Sylvester Till

Memories of
The Royal Electrical Mechanical Engineers WWII
My life as a soldier from 1939 to Demob in August 1946

Chapter 1
Basic Training

Prior to 1939 things were very unsettled in Europe with Adolph Hitler and Nazi Germany, and in early 1939 the British Government passed a law for conscription to come into force, whereby all men born in 1919, aged 20, had to go into the Army for six months to do military service.

There was no option, and you could not choose whether you wanted to serve in the Royal Navy, Army or Royal Air Force, all had to go into the Army, and they put you in whichever Corps or Regiment they thought fit. I, along with my ex-school classmates from Freckleton School, all registered at Kirkham Labour Exchange in June 1939 for six months military service, which was called the Militia. Some were called up for training within two weeks of registering and didn't get out at the end of six months because the war had started on 3 September 1939, and they had to stay in for its full duration. I, along with all others from the same area, had to report to an old school in Pole Street, Preston for a medical, and it was there that they told you which Corps or

Regiment you had to go in. I was passed A1, and being a tradesman motor bodybuilder had to go into the Royal Army Ordnance Corps, which at that time maintained all the army required.

All this happened to me within a few days of war being declared on 3rd September 1939. At the time I worked at H.V. Burlingham Caravans, and as this was a luxury trade the Government commandeered all stock to be used on war work, and the company closed down with two months of war being declared, so I was out of work. I had tried everywhere to get work but as soon as a prospective employer knew I was twenty and registered for the Army they wouldn't employ me, saying I could well be called up the following week, which was true, of course.

Weeks went by and I wasn't called up, and at the end of six months I was still out of work. At this time, work had started on Kirkham RAF Camp, which is now the Open Prison and I managed to get a job working for Wimpey's as a labourer. They wouldn't give me a tradesman's position because I was a motor bodybuilder and not in the Joiner's Union. So there I was labouring for some of the joiners and I could have done their job ten times better myself. Anyway, it was a job and better than being out of work. It was good pay too.

I worked for six months on the RAF Camp and by that time H.V. Burlingham's Caravans had started doing war work again making trailer canteens and trailer ambulances for bombed areas, so I went back there to work. I remember the boss H.V. Burlingham would not pay me full tradesman's rate, which was one shilling and eight pence an hour, which would be about eight and a half pence in today's money, because I hadn't enough experience. He offered me one shilling an hour, five pence in today's money. I took the job and had to travel all the way to Garstang for that, about 19 miles. People today get money for old rope, and are nowhere near as skilled as tradesmen of that day. Today's tradesmen would have been kicked out for the work they turn out.

After another six months I still hadn't been called up and I felt sure they had forgotten me, so I asked the boss H.V. Burlingham for the full rate of pay, and he agreed to this. Then in April 1941 I got my call up papers along with His Majesty's Shilling for me to report to Royal Army Ordnance Corps, Lannion Barracks, Pembroke Dock, South Wales. It was April 24th 1941 and I remember the day well. I caught the Ribble bus to Preston at about 8 o'clock in order to catch a train at Preston about 9 o'clock to take me to Crewe, where I had to change to a train going directly to Pembroke Dock. I remember it was Thursday, which was call up day for the Army. I boarded the Pembroke train with hundreds of other young men, with our little suitcases to send our civilian clothes back home. Little did I know how many thousands and thousands of miles I would travel by land and sea in the next five and a half years. I am sure all the other young men were thinking the same as me, *What will it be like to become a soldier in the army?*

We were soon to find out; I only remember the name of one station as we travelled down from Crewe, it was called Llandilo. It was a single track line and we had to wait for the train coming up the line to give our driver a big brass key, like a piece of tube, before our train could move down the single track line. Having never been away from home much this was exploration indeed.

Eventually we arrived at Pembroke Dock station about 4 o'clock. We were met by a sergeant, formed up in threes, and marched through the town, which was about as big as Lytham, to the entrance to Lannion Barracks. It was a beautiful afternoon and we were each given an army

Call-up group, Lannion Barracks, Pembroke Dock, April 24th 1941

number, mine was 10551900, along with a knife, fork, spoon and enamel cup, if you were lucky. I got a tin basin to drink out of, which I used until I eventually went abroad and was issued with a cup. We were then marched up to the barrack room and put in a company. I was in C Company. We were then given a thing like a sack to fill with straw for a bed and were allocated double tier bunks; I was in the top one.

There were about thirty-six men in our barrack room, all came from the London area except for two who came from Northumberland, one from Scotland and me from Lancashire. The sergeant in charge of us was Sergeant Hyde from Manchester. We all then went to the cookhouse for our tea. I remember it was stew, and rough at that. Some of the chaps wouldn't eat it, but after about three days drilling they were ravenous enough to eat a horse. As I went to bed that first night I couldn't help thinking about the soft comfortable bed I had slept in the night before. I suppose everyone was thinking the same. It was no use dwelling on what had been our life before, we were now to be trained as soldiers, and reveille was at 6am.

We were the first company out for PT – Physical Training. It was a bit chilly in shorts and vest at 6am, but it was a lovely morning, in fact it was lovely and sunny all the time we were at Pembroke Dock. We were there for a month, by which time we were supposed to be fully trained soldiers. Of course it was concentrated infantry training from 6am to about 5pm every day with the infantry weapons. We had to learn how to use rifles, machine guns, Tommy guns, grenades, sticky bombs etc., It was hard going at first until we got limbered up. It was amazing how smart all the young men were at the end of four weeks, when a passing out parade was held on the barrack square with each company there to see each other do their stuff. The men were a great credit to the infantry NCO who had trained them from raw recruits, a month previous to that they didn't even know their left from their right.

I remember one rough night we had when the whole company was "jolloped" - in other words the cook had put something in the food to move our bowels, and move we did, at about midnight. I remember I had stomach-ache and got up to go to the toilets on the landing only to find them full and chaps waiting in a queue. I dashed down the stone stairs along with scores of other men, and ran across the parade ground to a hut with about fifteen toilets in, but these were also full and with men waiting. I managed to hold on

7

until a toilet was vacant but some men couldn't hold on. You can imagine the mess, and more men were coming in all the time, hundreds of them. The following morning we were given buckets and long brushes to clear up the trail which started on the stone steps of the barrack room, and went right across the parade ground to the other toilets where men had been unable to make it to the toilets. I bet the NCO instructors were having a laugh that night. We didn't think it funny!

About midnight on the Sunday night of our second week the Germans bombed us at Pembroke Dock. The raid lasted about three hours. We had to get out of our barracks into slit trenches, which had already been dug, and led down to the sea.

Of course Pembroke Dock was a real garrisoned town with our barracks on the edge of the town, a street away. On the other side of the dock was the Royal Artillery Barracks. There were cargo ships already in the dock and Royal Navy ships came in to refuel from scores of fuel tanks to one side of our barracks. Royal Air Force Sunderland Flying Boats took off from the dock on U-boat patrol, so I suppose the Germans had good reason to bomb it. These raids went on every night for the next two weeks after that until our training finished. They hit the dock quite a lot, but sadly the town was badly hit too. I think about 65 civilians were killed. We had to take it in turns in between training to go into the town and dig amongst the damaged property. At the end of four weeks we had been well trained but were glad to get away to our next destination to be tested for our skills as craftsmen, and also to get a decent night's rest.

We left Pembroke Dock as trained soldiers at about 8 o'clock on the Sunday night by train to travel all night to a place called Gopsall Hall, Twycross, in Warwickshire. The nearest railway station to Twycross was Ashby de la Zouch. I remember we had to change at Gloucester at about 2am on the Monday morning, and wait until 4am for a train to Ashby de la Zouch, arriving at about 6am, in pouring rain, a big change from beautiful sunshine at Pembroke Dock. Trucks arrived at the station to take us to Gopsall Hall, Twycross, about 7 miles away. The Hall had been a gentleman's residence but had been commandeered by the government for an army camp made up of bell tents in the grounds. The Hall was the Officers' Quarters. I will never forget our reception as we paraded wet and tired in that grey morning rain at about 7am in front of the main entrance to the Hall.

The camp Adjutant stood three flights up on the stone step entrance to tell us this was Gopsall Hall, and if any of us had any ideas of deserting this God-forsaken place, it was a mile to the nearest perimeter gate then three miles to the nearest bus stop, so we could forget it. He went on to tell us that we would be there at least six weeks, depending on whether we passed our trade tests as craftsmen.

After the speech by the Adjutant, we were then taken to the bell tents, which already had men in them. The Sergeant in charge pulled a tent flap up and said, "two in here", then on to the next tent, "three in here" and so on until he had got rid of about sixty men. I well remember being put in a tent which already had nine men and their kit in it and I had to set myself out with my blanket under the tent flap. Of course, when the men came in or went out I sometimes got stood on, and if it was raining, which it was for about half of the time, then my blanket and kit got wet. I remember I caught a terrible cold, it was my first experience of living in a tent and I wasn't too thrilled about it.

Half our time was spent making roads and footpaths around the tents and we carried all the old used bricks by hand to make them. The other half of our time was spent having trade tests, both practical and theory, in order that we could be graded into first, second, or third class craftsmen. Half a crown a day, twelve and a half pence in today's money, was an ordinary soldier's pay. Third class craftsmen went up to three shillings and sixpence a day, second class was four shillings a day, and first class, which I managed to achieve, went up to five shillings a day - twenty five pence in today's money, quite an improvement on half a crown.

I remember one young lad I got to know called Gibson, from Hoole near Preston, who had served his apprenticeship at Todkills Motor Bodybuilders in Preston. He got the same practical test as I did which was to dovetail a drawer, a different job altogether from motor bodybuilding. He said to me that he hadn't got a clue how to set the dovetails out, let alone how to cut them. Fortunately for us both I had done some dovetailing so I told him I would set them out, show him how to cut them and help him glue them up. When he got his marks he passed second class and was quite thrilled about it. I never saw him again after we left Gopsall Hall although I made enquiries about him at Todkills Motor Bodybuilders in Preston after the war. I think he returned to Leyland Motors, so we lost touch.

Gopsall Hall was a big awakening for us, I remember the toilets were a few wooden posts driven into the ground with sacking nailed on to form the back, and the partitions dividing each toilet were just sacking. The door was a piece of sack nailed at the top, left to hang down and corrugated iron formed the roof. The toilet was a bucket with a board with a hole in it on top. A gang of Pioneer Corps men came around every day with a low-loading wagon to empty the buckets, and I was glad not to be one of them.

I remember doing my first guard duty at the entrance to Gopsall Hall, known to us as Gospel Hall. I only went out of the place once. It was a mile to walk to the gate to get onto the road and three miles to the nearest bus stop to get into a little town called Measham. By the time I had walked the four miles from the bus stop to the camp I never wanted to go out again. We did get several local concert parties out to entertain us and they were all very talented.

After about six weeks I was sent with about forty other chaps to Stirling, Scotland. It was a Saturday when we left Gopsall Hall for Ashby de la Zouch railway station. We arrived at Glasgow Central Station about 7pm and had to change stations to Buchanan Street Station. The Corporal in charge of us didn't know where Buchanan Street Station was, however, we had several Scots lads with us. One said he knew the way so the Corporal put him in the front rank to show us the way. After marching around for about an hour in Glasgow on a Saturday night the Scots lad said he was lost, so it was like the song, *"I belong to Glasgow"*.

After several enquiries from civilians we arrived at Buchanan Street Station at about 9pm. When we arrived at Stirling at about 9.45pm we were tired out. We were then taken in trucks to a camp made up of wooden huts. This was not far from Stirling Castle. On the Sunday our documentation was sorted out. On the Monday we had to go to Stirling Castle for a medical inspection, then it was back to camp and into workshops. I remember on a clear day we could see the Firth of Forth Bridge in the distance from our camp.

I was only at Stirling for two weeks before being sent with twelve other men to a little place called Bonhill, about three miles from Dumbarton and about three miles from Balloch at the foot of Loch Lomond. In between Bonhill and Loch Lomond was a little place called Alexandria. Our camp was situated just outside Bonhill on the back road to Dumbarton, in a field sloping down to the River Leven. We were now in bell tents again and I remember the names of the men, Ernie McMurdy from London, Ernie Palmer from Great Yarmouth, Tom Symes from Somerset, George from

Sylvester Till aged 22, six months after call-up

Droylesden, Manchester, and me from Freckleton. We were all about 21 or 22 and all either joiners or motor bodybuilders. Ernie Palmer was the youngest at nineteen, and the tales they told when they came in at night about their experiences with the local girls, I wouldn't repeat.

I remember them all very well, especially George. He was the smallest of us all and what he daren't do wasn't worth doing. He always overstayed his leave by at least a day or two. Of course, when he did turn up he was always on a charge, absent without leave, and he usually got about three days jankers confined to barracks, but he said it was worth it for another day at home. He always had some good tales to tell after going out with some girl. One night when he came in the tent Tom Symes said, 'What have you been up to tonight George?'

George said, 'I met up with that ginger haired girl Mary that waves to us as we march down.'

Of course Tom wanted more detail, 'Where did you go George?'

'She knew a place like a barn up Jamestown way.'

George said, 'How did you go on with her?'

Tom asked, 'Was she alright?'

'Was she alright?' George repeated.

15

'I'd say she was, and she had lovely child-bearing hips.'

Tom wanted more detail, he wouldn't let it drop, so George gave us a first hand report, but I can't repeat it here. Suffice it to say that George certainly educated us with the stories of his exploits, and he always gave us a laugh.

The last time I saw George was before he went on leave, and he didn't want to take all his kit with him so he asked me to keep his spare pair of boots in my kit bag. This was dodgy for me because if whilst he was away there had been a kit inspection and I was found with an extra pair of boots, which I wasn't supposed to have, I would have been on a charge for stealing. However, there was no kit inspection but George overstayed his leave as usual and was put in the guardroom. When I came back from workshops George had been posted somewhere else, which left me saddled with his boots. I heard that he had been sent to Stirling Depot, so I wrapped his boots up in brown paper and smuggled them out of camp and posted them by Royal Mail to Stirling. Whether he ever got them I never heard, he probably ended up on another charge for losing army kit. Knowing George I'm sure he would survive, although I think he will be in the guardroom in the sky now, knowing his lifestyle.

Our army workshops were in a disused dye factory called Dillichip Mill where they used to dye silk woven in the area. It is still there today. The last time I was in Bonhill, in 1992, I had a walk down Dillichip Lawn or Lane where we used to march down to our workshops and where George met up with the girl with the lovely child-bearing hips. It looked just the same, but I wasn't allowed through the gates because it had become a whisky distillery or whisky storage place.

I met and made some good friends whilst at Bonhill. Two good friends to me were James and Connie McEwan whom I met at Alexandria Church. Connie came from Bolton in Lancashire so we had a lot in common. After demob I went up to Scotland to see them. By this time they had two children. The next time I went up there they had moved to somewhere in England so I lost touch with them.

Whilst stationed at Bonhill a new regiment was formed called Royal Electrical Mechanical Engineers, or REME for short. I, along with all other tradesmen were transferred into REME from the Royal Army Ordnance Corps, in about late 1941. Of course, when I arrived at Bonhill it was August 1941 and being under canvas wasn't too bad then, although by November it was getting very cold at night. We had no proper water supply, just a spring, which ran out of the rocks at the side of Dumbarton Road. We had to get water in our mess tins from the spring then run back to camp for a wash and shave. I remember there was a great big mirror in a wooden frame hanging from a tree with two ropes, which we used for shaving. There was no protection from the wind and rain, we just got washed and shaved in the rain with our capes on. We were all living in the same conditions, so just moaned and got on with it until we had an epidemic of sore throats and had to gargle each morning with Condies Fluid, provided in buckets.

The cooks had to do all the cooking from the spring water at the side of the Dumbarton Road, so everything was pretty basic. We had to march down to our workshops every morning, about one mile away, then march back at twelve for dinner, march back after dinner, finish work at 6pm and march back for tea. On dark mornings and evenings someone carried a clear glass storm lantern in front and someone carried a red painted glass storm lantern at the rear in order that vehicles did not mow us down. On top of this we had guard duty or fire picket at camp and workshops, and all day Saturday was the same as every other working day.

Eventually, as sore throats worsened, a store shed at our works was cleared out and we were all billeted in there, which was snug, warm and dry, whilst a new camp of Nissan huts was built for us with proper washing and toilet facilities, this was in 1942.

There is another incident I remember well at Bonhill. Being tradesmen our job was to repair all vehicles, tanks, guns etc., and keep them on the move so we didn't get a lot of regimental exercise after our first month of infantry training, yet we were always told we were soldiers first and tradesmen after. Unfortunately the workshop officers wanted the work turning out and the regimental officers wanted us to be soldiers, it was like serving two masters. On this particular occasion the regimental officers wanted about 40 men, so many out of each workshop, to go on a cross country exercise. Whenever we got these regimental stunts it had to be in our own time, so it was always in the evening or on a Sunday, our day off. I was included in this stunt and had to parade at 8am on Sunday morning, properly dressed with webbing equipment, great packs, respirators at the alert (on our chests), rifles and steel helmets.

We were inspected on parade before setting off by Company Sergeant Major Fraser, a Scotsman, about fifty with First World War medal ribbons. He was dressed the same as us, no rifle, although he had a revolver in his holster. After inspection we marched out of camp on the Sunday morning with the Sergeant Major in command. We marched down into Bonhill Village, over Bonhill Bridge over the River Leven, then straight through the main street in Alexandria and on to the village of Balloch at the foot of Loch Lomond. We were then halted in front of Balloch Park gates, which were of wrought iron, about 7 feet high and locked. We had probably marched about three or four miles, and there was hardly a soul about, after all it was Sunday morning, the milkman was delivering milk and the paper lads were on their rounds.

Sergeant Major Fraser tried the gates, but they were locked alright. At the other side of the gates a park workman was sweeping the drive and the Sergeant Major called to him to open the gates.

'I am not allowed to,' answered the workman, pointing to the notice board, which said, "we don't open until eleven". It was about 9 o'clock by then.

We were all stood to attention wondering what was going to happen when the Sergeant Major said, 'Look here my man, I want these gates open to bring these men through, regardless of your opening time.'

The workman said, 'I can't let you through, it's against the regulations.'

We were all listening wondering what was going to happen next. The Sergeant Major then said, 'Is the Park Superintendent about? If he is, get him here.'

The workman then went to an office, which looked a bit like a lodge at one side of the gate, and got the Park Superintendent out.

The Superintendent said, 'What can I do for you?'

The Sergeant Major replied, 'I want these gates opened to bring these guards through.' He called us guards although we were only workshop soldiers, although I suppose we looked the part with rifles and steel helmets on.

The Park Superintendent replied that it was against the regulations, they were not allowed to open before 11 o'clock, it was on the notice board.

We were all enjoying the confrontation but Sergeant Major Fraser wasn't going to give up. He said to the Superintendent, 'This country is under martial law, I will give you twenty seconds to open these gates in the King's name, to let the King's men through. If you don't I will blow the bloody lock off, put you under arrest and march you back to barracks, escorted by two of these guards.'

We waited and wondered what he was going to use to blow the lock off as we hadn't a round of ammunition amongst us. Anyway, the bluff worked, the Superintendent got the keys and opened the gates to let us through, and even though it was Sunday morning and our day off work, I'm glad I was there to see that bluff work. We went straight through the park, over the perimeter hedge and onto the hills, marching our way round back towards camp for dinner.

The story went round after this Sunday exercise and bluff that Sergeant Major Fraser had a bet on with another Sergeant Major that he would get a squad of men through Balloch Park before the gates were officially open, and he did it with forty men to prove it. They are not the same gates now at Balloch Park but there are gates on with a notice board stating opening times. I have stood in front of them several times since then, remembering that Sunday morning with Sergeant Major Fraser addressing us as guards and bluffing his way through. I am sure by now that Sergeant Major Fraser will be on the great parade ground in the sky, where I am sure St Peter will have opened the gates for him.

I liked being at Bonhill and one of my workshop mates was a lad called Joe Lickerish, he was a Scot from Stirling. He married a local girl from Jamestown called Betty McPhearson. Sadly the day came, on the very day I was scheduled for ten day's home leave, when I was put on an overseas draft and had to join 23 Workshop Company, REME, being mobbed up at Nottingham. I remember it well. Sergeant Fears, our shop NCO, told me to hand my tools in and get back to camp to collect all my kit, it was about 2.30pm, all rather a rush. I had to report to Sergeant Major Fraser to collect all my documentation, travel warrant, route to be taken, times of trains, etc. When I reported to him he said, 'I'm sorry about this laddie, you were going on leave today.'

When I looked at my route I had to go via Glasgow, Edinburgh and Grantham to Nottingham. I asked the Sergeant Major if he could make my route via Glasgow, Preston and Crewe to Nottingham, then I could perhaps get home for 3 or 4 hours if I got to Preston. My family were expecting me home on leave the following morning and I had no way of letting them know I was on a draft. Sergeant Major replied that he could not alter the route but told me that once I got through the camp gate I could go where I liked. 'I know what I would do,' the Sergeant Major said, 'see if you can get the railway ticket clerk to make your ticket out via Glasgow, Preston, Crewe and Nottingham.' He then shook hands with me and wished me the best of luck.

I got on the truck to take me to Alexandria Bonhill Station. I explained to the ticket clerk what the situation was and he said, 'I am not supposed to do this, but under the circumstances I will make your ticket out via the route you request.' I thanked him and got on the train to Glasgow, then got a train to Preston at about 10.30pm, the same train I would have caught to go on leave. I arrived in Preston about 5am, put all my kit in the left luggage office and legged it up to the bus station to get the 6am bus to Freckleton. I got home about 6.30am. I told them I was on a draft and could only stay until dinnertime because my train left Preston for Crewe at 1pm. It was very disappointing but that was soldiering.

After I'd had my dinner I went to catch a bus for Preston at 12pm. When it arrived it was full with people standing so I couldn't get on and there were no more buses due until 1 o'clock, but whilst I was waiting a lorry came along and I thumbed a lift. He said he was going to Liverpool and I asked him if he would drop me at Penwortham Bridge, which is what he did. I thanked him and nearly ran all the way up Fishergate Hill to the railway station. I got my kit out of the left luggage department and the train to Crewe was at the platform. I just jumped aboard as the guard blew his whistle. Off I went, changing at Crewe for a Nottingham train. I think it was the slowest train I was ever on, stopping at every little village station every 3 or 4 miles across country to Nottingham. As we chugged along the sun set and dusk came to end that October day. Then came blackout, with all lights blacked out.

We arrived at Nottingham about 7 o'clock. The address I had to report to was 23 Workshop Company REME, Nottingham. As I hadn't kept to my proper route by going via Preston I daren't ask the military police on the station where this company was in case they checked my documents and found I hadn't kept to the route I had been given, and by now I was about 12 hours overdue. I should have been in Nottingham at 6am and was therefore absent without leave. I daren't go to the Railway Transport Officer for the same reason, I would have been arrested and put on a charge, so I came off the station to the forecourt and asked a taxi driver if he knew the whereabouts of the company. He said he didn't but told me to ask one of the bus drivers. Neither drivers nor conductors knew where it was but one conductor said that there was a camp on his route that might be the one. I got on the bus with all lights dimmed and we headed out of Nottingham into the countryside. It was a pitch-black night, no moon or stars.

After we had been going slowly along for about 45 minutes the conductor came to me and said that he couldn't see very well in the blackout but we should be somewhere near the camp now. The bus stopped and I got off with all my kit, greatcoat, great pack, small pack, respirator, steel helmet and kit bag. I waited until my eyes got accustomed to the dark and the bus disappeared in the distance. It was so dark I couldn't see the hedge across the road. There wasn't a glimmer of light or sound of anything as I sat there on my kit bag. I was lost, tired and hungry, having worked all the previous day, travelled all the previous night, travelled all this day and it was now nearly 9pm. As I sat there on my kit bag, I wondered which way to walk because whichever way I went I could have been walking away from the camp. As I sat, the words of the old hymn came to mind,

"Lead kindly light amidst the encircling gloom.
Lead thou me on.

The night is dark and I am far from home,
Lead thou me on."

Then I heard some women's voices coming nearer as I sat on my kit bag against the hedge. As they drew near I stood up and said, 'Excuse me.'

'Oh my God,' they said, 'we'd never have seen you. Are you lost?'

I asked them if there was a camp nearby. They said there was and told me to follow them about half a mile in some woods; I followed. They sounded like middle-aged women as one said to the other, 'It's a shame how they send these young lads out at all hours looking for camps, we get many a lot of them knocking on our door asking for directions at night. I've a good mind to write to Churchill about it.'

I said, 'Mrs, you don't know one half, I've been travelling all last night from Scotland and all day today, and I still don't know where I'm sleeping tonight.'

We got to the wood and the women told me that the camp was down the lane. I thanked them and said goodnight. They wished me good luck and off they went. As they left, a Corporal going down the lane said, 'Are you lost mate?' I told him that I was looking for a 23 Workshop Company REME. He said, 'Well this isn't it, this is the

Royal Corps of Signals.' Then he said, 'You'd better come with me, there are two guards up here and they won't let you in because we have a password.'

We went along the lane together, then were halted by the guard shouting, 'Who goes there?'

The corporal replied, 'Friend.'

The reply was 'Advance and be recognised.'

The corporal went forward and explained the situation. The guard contacted the guardroom in a very strict and efficient manner. It would be about 9.30pm by this time. I was taken to the cookhouse for a cup of tea and corned beef sandwich then they found me a bed for the night. That day was 23rd October 1942 and unbeknown to me or anyone else it was the night of the start of the battle of El Alamein on the western desert and the beginning of the end of the war in North Africa and a start towards the end of Nazi Germany.

I didn't sleep much that night in a strange camp and not knowing anyone. The following morning after breakfast I had to report to the Signals Company Office. There were about five other men who had landed up there looking for 23 Workshop Company REME that night. They found out this Company was being mobbed up at a little place called

Carlton, about three miles outside Nottingham. A truck was laid on and we were driven to Carlton Drill Hall, which was to be our headquarters and training ground for the next seven weeks. We were all billeted in different halls or Sunday Schools. I was in the Co-Op Hall.

Each day we all had to make our own way to the Drill Hall to parade on the cobbled street for roll call, then it was intense infantry training and infantry weapons and night exercises. At the end of six weeks training we got seven days embarkation leave.

The 23 Workshop Company had been mustered up in dribs and drabs from all over the British Isles. I landed up from Scotland on my own, others came in ones and twos, threes, sixes, twenties and so on, all in different trades, engineers, panel beaters, tinsmiths, coppersmiths, blacksmiths, motor mechanics, driver mechanics, painters, sign writers, moulders, pattern makers, tent makers, joiners, motor bodybuilders, auto electricians, instrument makers, clock makers, toolmakers, lathe machinists, wood machinists, in fact you mention a trade we had them. All told, there were about 400 Officers, Warrant Officers, NCOs and other ranks, and even though I didn't know anyone at first, by the time I had trained, paraded several times a day with a different man either side of me every day, I knew most of the names or nicknames. The following always sticks in my mind:

We had finished our training and half the company had been sent on seven days' embarkation leave. I was in the second half to go. We got the bus to Nottingham with all our kit, and then the train to Manchester where we had to change stations. A bus went between Victoria Station and Piccadilly Station for troops only and one of the lads with us, I never knew his name, was nicknamed Rommel. He was about the same build as me, five feet ten or eleven and he looked a bit like Rommel the German Field Marshall. It seemed he lived somewhere on the route the bus was going along in Manchester. I remember he asked the driver if he would stop at a certain street to let him get off with all his kit. The driver said he wasn't allowed to stop between stations but he would slow down near the street to allow him to jump off whilst the bus was still going. I remember him well, his greatcoat on, great pack on his back, and kit bag over his shoulder, as he waited on the bus platform getting ready to jump off. The bus slowed down a bit and Rommel jumped, his hob-nailed boots making sparks on the stone street sets. He did a bit of a wobble, nearly losing his balance, then recovered and went marching along the footpath as the bus sped on. I found out later that he was married and had two little girls, and little did I think, nor him either as he went happily on leave, as I will relate later, it would be the last time his young wife and two little girls would ever see him. He would have been in his early twenties, the same as me.

The seven days leave soon seemed to pass. Then it was goodbye and back on the bus and train to Nottingham, then Carlton. We had completed our training course so the next day or so was spent getting kitted out with tropical kit with an extra kit bag. On Friday 11 December the local talent organised a farewell concert for us in the Methodist Sunday School and it was a first class performance. The last turn, I always remember, it is imprinted in my memory, was a lady singing a song with the words, *"Vilia, Oh Vilia, The Witch of the Woods"*. It was a well-known song by Franz Lehár, from the operetta *The Merry Widow*. It was beautiful to listen to, and even though the room was full of soldiers in their hob-nailed boots, you could have heard a pin drop as they listened to the lady singing that song. Whenever I hear it I think of that farewell concert at Carlton Methodist Sunday School room. A lovely memory.

The next day was Saturday and our last night out, because on Sunday 13 December 1942 we had to assemble with all our kit at the drill hall where we were confined to barracks until Sunday evening when we paraded for the last time at six o'clock on the cobbled street in front of the drill hall. There was a roll call at about 6.30pm and then we set off to march the three miles to Nottingham railway station. Being December it was dark and a soldier in the front rank carried a clear storm lantern. Someone at the rear carried a red one. All our kit had gone to the station on a truck. We got to the station about 8 o'clock and the train was waiting at the platform. We were told to board it, to fill each compartment and to pull down the blinds.

At about 9pm the train pulled out and we were on our way to an unknown destination. As the train slowed down to go through a station we peeped round the edge of the blind and saw the station was York, so we were going north somewhere. The night passed and daylight broke so we were able to raise the blinds, and we found by the station names that we were in Scotland, no doubt heading for the Clyde, and sure enough, by midday the train pulled up on the dock side at Gouroch. There were ferryboats waiting to take us out to the troopship *"Britannic"* which was anchored in the middle of the Clyde. All our kit had been dumped on the dockside from the train so we had to find our kit bags, etc., all named and numbered, then get on board the ferry.

Troopship Britannic III at anchor off Hunters Quay, Dunoon, Firth of Clyde, Scotland.

Chapter 2
Embarkation

After a few minutes ferry trip we were boarding the *"Britannic"*, which looked massive in comparison to the ferryboat. We were then guided along gangways and stairs to our various mess decks. I was on "D" Deck, going towards the bows of the ship, I think the mess deck number was 20. Everything had been gutted out of the ship as it had been a passenger liner, and all the decks were fitted out with long fixed wooden tables with fixed wooden seats on either side. There was nothing else except hooks to hang hammocks on if you wished to sleep that way. Other than that you slept either on the table or floor, neither were very comfortable, it was a matter of getting to sleep where you could with 7,000 troops on board a liner built for 1,000 passengers.

We had to take all our kit down into the holds to give us more room, except for small pack containing a clean shirt, vest, underpants, socks, washing and shaving equipment; that was Monday 14 December 1942. On Tuesday 15 December we were issued with life jackets and had to attend boat drill on promenade deck opposite our lifeboats. This procedure was carried out every day throughout our voyage.

Whilst we were at boat stations from 9am to 10am the ship was inspected on every deck from stem to stern by ships officers to ensure that it was clean and tidy.

After boat drill if we weren't on guard on fire picket duty, we explored the ship and engine rooms. The rest of the day was spent either reading or playing cards, concert parties were formed, choirs and musical entertainment, and brains trusts were formed. Sometimes we would attend lectures, perhaps about railways, the Royal Navy or some other interesting subject. It was surprising how much talent there was amongst 7,000 men and women, because there were some Queen Alexandra's Nurses on board too. Of course, they were always on "A" Deck, the top deck, with officers.

All these activities were being formed whilst we were anchored in mid Clyde, and in the early hours of the morning, about 2am on Friday 18 December 1942, I awoke to hear the ship's engines running, so I knew we were under way. When daylight came we could see the distant hills of Scotland as we headed into the Irish Sea and Atlantic Ocean, and one could feel a slight swell on the sea. No doubt we were all wondering when, if ever, we would see the British Isles again. Some didn't. As the day went on the weather grew worse and by teatime there was quite a storm brewing, and most of us were either being sick or feeling sick. I was never seasick but felt awful and just wanted to lie down. As the ship rocked from stem to stern it was rolling from side to side, which was the worst, and I remember our tea being brought down in containers from the galley, it was pork chops and baked beans, but just to look at it made us feel sick. There were only about three men on our mess deck who could face it and they had a right tuck-in. The rest of it went back to the galley waste and overboard. The storm just worsened as night came on and it was bad for about a week; for the first three nights we were told to keep our clothes on. By Sunday I, along with others, were feeling better and starting to eat, I suppose we had now got our sea legs. No matter what ship I was on after that I was never seasick again, mind you, it was never as rough as that first week in the Atlantic Ocean over Christmas in December 1942.

Toilets on the *Britannic* (and other troopships) were pretty basic, and considering that there were 7,000 bowels to clear every day it was amazing how we coped. Our mess deck toilet was a plank with twenty holes in a row, just a partition between each hole, no front on at all, so no privacy, and no matter what time you went, day or night, there were always men there. There was no flushing but salt water was flushed underneath through a trough. When it was stormy and the ship rocked stem to stern the water swished to one end or the other, so it was wise if possible not to get on the end holes or you got wet. Of course, all fresh water was rationed on troopships. It was turned on at 6am for washing and shaving, turned off at 8.30am and turned on again at 4pm and turned off at 6pm. We could have a shower in saltwater using saltwater soap.

On Christmas Day I remember as we stood at boat stations from 9am to 10am, one of the Royal Navy Corvettes escorting us sailed between the convoy of ships and hailed us though a megaphone, 'The Captain and crew of *HMS Quilliam* wish Captain, crew and troops of *Britannic* a very Merry Christmas.' The Corvette looked so small as it tossed about in the storm, far worse than our ship, which seemed to do everything except capsize.

There was a church service on Christmas Day with carols, then a concert by some of the lads in the afternoon. On Sunday evening there was community hymn singing in what had previously been the ballroom. As we headed south west the weather improved, the hymn singing was held aft on the open deck. We could often hear the men on other

HMS Quilliam
Escort from Clyde to Freetown, then Durban 1942 - 1943

troopships singing their hymns as the sound drifted across on the breeze. So that was Christmas on a troopship!

We sailed on and of course we always knew when there were German U-boats about. The *Britannic* was the flagship for the convoy. Semaphore signs with flags or Aldis Lamps signals were sent from our ship to the rest of the convoy. If there were U-boats about the whole convoy would have to zigzag so that they could not get a fix on a target. The zigzagging would usually start at dusk and sometimes go on all night until dawn. It was controlled from our ship, one blast on the foghorn was the signal for the whole convoy to alter course so many degrees to port for a period of fifteen minutes, then the horn would sound again for two blasts. This told the whole convoy to alter course so many degrees to starboard for fifteen minutes. This would go on all night whilst the horn kept blowing or until the danger was passed. The nights were often pitch black, there were no lights on any ships and it was amazing to see as the dawn broke how all the ships had kept their positions, they must have kept a very good look out. Of course, we didn't get much sleep with the foghorn blowing every fifteen minutes all through the night, but we never lost any ships.

Eventually we altered course South East and steamed towards West Africa. On New Year's Eve afternoon we anchored close inshore to Freetown in order to replenish fresh water and fuel. I remember at midnight all the ship's bells rang and all the natives on shore were singing and dancing as the New Year came in. During the daytime native boys swam out to our ship and waited for us to throw coins in the water, which they then dived down for. Silver coins were the best to see. After all the ships had been replenished from lighters, they assembled in convoy to proceed further.

The troopship *Britannic III* sailed from the Clyde, Scotland at 2am on the morning of December 18th 1942, to join ships to form a convoy somewhere in the Atlantic ocean. We were the flagship for the convoy, so *Britannic III* was at the centre. We had a good view of all ships, namely *Highland Brigade, Tarifa, Rangitikia, Britannic* 682 feet long, *Esperance Bay, Highland Princess, City of Lincoln, Orion, Matoroa*. I think most of the ships were troopships, so no doubt we had a good Royal Navy escort. These are some of the escort ships: *HMS Caernarfon Castle, HMS Cheshire, HMS Quilliam,* there were other Royal Navy ships on the horizon, no doubt checking some suspected German

U-boat position. The Commodore for the convoy on *Britannic III* was Rear Admiral A T Tillard DSO, Royal Navy Reserve.

As we left Freetown the weather was calm and sunny. Porpoises swam along with the ships, and flying fish skimmed over the waves. We ascertained that our next port of call would be either Capetown or Durban, South Africa. Our escort of destroyers changed as we left Freetown to *HMS Aliantara, HMS Cheshire, HMS Quilliam, HMS Rockwood, HMS Cyclamen and HMS Crocus.*

After two more weeks sailing we docked at Durban, and what a welcome there was. It seemed that whenever troopships docked a woman known as the "lady in white" came down to the docks, no matter what time of day or night, to sing to the troops on the ships. She was a beautiful singer and sang all manner of songs, from *There'll always be an England, Loch Lomond,* to *Roll out the barrel,* or *Wish me luck,* etc. I have found out from the library that she was called Perla Siedle Gibson, and she wrote a book called *The Lady in White.* I found it very interesting. Her husband and son were in the South African Forces, and even though her son was killed in Italy she still went down to the docks to sing to the convoys that came in, a very brave lady.

HMS Cyclamen - Convoy Escort from Freetown to Durban, Jan 1943.

HMS Crocus – Convoy Escort from Freetown to Durban, 1943.

We got off the *Britannic,* which had been our home for a month, and had to march through Durban to a transit camp to await another ship to take us wherever we were going, which we still didn't know.

The transit camp was about two miles outside Durban in a clearing in a wood. I remember there were monkeys playing about in the trees, they never seemed to come down. The camp was made up of tents in rows opposite each other. We had very little to do apart from guard duty, and keeping the camp tidy and clean.

Chapter 3
Durban

There was a shop in the camp which opened every day selling all sorts of delicious fruit, bananas, peaches, apples, grapes, pears and pineapples. We could get a whole pineapple for about twopence. We were allowed out of camp every afternoon after 12 o'clock, providing one soldier stayed in to watch the tent and the tent opposite which had our kit in, so we took turns at staying in.

The buses were all free to ride in and we found Durban to be a town of luxury. There were canteens for us to use to get a meal for a shilling and these comprised some of the following: bacon, eggs, sausages, steak, chops, vegetables, all manner of sweets, sundaes, trifle, cream, ice cream, and all of this with no rationing at all! The sun shone every day, there were swimming pools and no blackout at night. It was really a place to remember!

One afternoon I decided to stay in camp and one of the lads in the tent opposite was supposed to stay behind to look after the two tents, so I went across to tell him that if he could sort it out with the guardroom I would see to the tents and he could go into Durban. He jumped at the offer and off he went. This same lad happened to be the one nick-named

Rommel, who I mentioned earlier, the one who jumped off the bus in Manchester as he went on embarkation leave to see his young wife and two little girls. Little did I think as he left to go into Durban what would happen to him in the next couple of years. It was a lovely holiday in Durban, a month of good things which was never to be repeated. Concerts were laid on for us too; little did we know what was to come.

Chapter 4
Further Troopship Experiences

Of course, all good things come to an end and a month of pleasure came to a halt one Sunday about the middle of February when trucks were laid on to take us down to Durban Docks to board the troopship *Felix Roussel*, a much smaller ship than the *Britannic*. It was a French ship and really scruffy. Moored alongside us was the cruiser HMS Dauntless, our convoy escort the following morning to another unknown destination.

It was a beautiful sunny Sunday night as we looked down over the rails at the cruiser. The Royal Marine Band had assembled aft to carry out the ceremony of Sunset, when the band plays as they lower the white ensign. They finished by playing that simple well-known hymn *"Now the Day is Over"*. One could hardly imagine as this lovely old hymn was played that there was a war on, yet so many happy memories.

The *Felix Roussel* was 575 feet long and weighed 17,000 tons, a much smaller ship than the *Britannic* which was 682 feet long and weighed 27,000 tons. It was built in 1930 at St Nazaine, France and taken over by the War

Troopship Felix Roussel – French passenger ship in peacetime.

49

HMS Dauntless,
Cruiser Convoy Escort, from Durban, South Africa to Bombay, India.

Department in 1941. It was returned to French ownership after the war.

On Monday morning, the day after we embarked, we left Durban docks at about 7am, with four other ships and our escort HMS Dauntless. We sailed for about five hours, probably about sixty miles out from Durban, when our engine stopped. There was immediate flashing of Aldis lamp signals to HMS Dauntless to inform them of the problem. Of course, when anything like this happens in a convoy, the rest of the convoy carries on at a slower speed and one of the escort ships cruises around to protect the stricken ship, but in this case we only had one escort ship and she had to look after the rest of the convoy in case of a U boat attack. But HMS Dauntless had a good turn of speed and kept coming back to us, no doubt to see if we were still afloat as we were a sitting target for U boats. However, after about four hours the engines started to turn over and after several more hours we caught up with the convoy, during the night.

Sadly, at about 5am the engines packed up again, and once more the convoy left us, a sitting duck in mid Indian Ocean. We understood it to be a bearing causing the trouble and we were stuck there floundering for almost ten hours with the Dauntless chasing back to us as often as she was able.

At last, at about 5pm we were on the move again and caught up with the convoy the following morning. We then steamed further up the Indian Ocean then steamed west towards Mombassa, East Africa, to discharge about fifteen persons. We stood off Mombassa as a boat was lowered to take the people ashore, and when it returned it was hoisted up on the davits, and we were on our way across the Indian Ocean, east to Bombay. We docked at Bombay about two weeks after leaving Durban. Half the troops were allowed into Bombay but I was in the half that had to stay on board ship so I never saw that city.

The following morning we disembarked and marched along the dock to another ship called the *Cap St Jacques*, another French ship taken over by the War Department. It was much smaller again, 417 feet long and weighing 8,000 tons. It had been a cargo ship but was now used for troops. We were in the ship's cargo hold and it felt like a convict ship. The sun shone through the holes in the grating above, which also let air in.

We set sail the same day, alone with no escort, still not knowing our destination, and we sailed still further up the

Troopship Gap St. Jaques, French cargo ship during peacetime.

Indian Ocean heading for the Arabian Sea. I remember on this ship I was on guard duty on the starboard side of the bridge, with another soldier on the port side, and the ship's Officer on the bridge came to tell me what I had to look out for. If I saw a silver streak coming towards us I was to give him a shout as it would be a torpedo from a U boat. However, the night passed without incident and this was the only time I was ever on the bridge of a ship.

We sailed through the Arabian Sea through the Straits of Hormuz, which is very narrow and separates Saudi Arabia from Persia (or Iran as it is now called). Once we were through the Straits into the Persian Gulf we knew our destination was to be Saudi Arabia, Persia or Iraq. We had sailed over the equator twice now, but it never seemed as hot as going up the Persian Gulf.

On we sailed, the sea like a millpond, until we were as far up the Gulf as we could go. Obviously our destination was Iraq. We left the Gulf to enter the Shatt Al Arab waterway which is the estuary to the rivers Euphrates and Tigris, and on to the port of Basra. All these names are mentioned in the Old Testament of *The Bible*, including Mesopotamia, which is Iraq. I remember as we sailed up the Shatt Al Arab waterway that it became much narrower with a date palm plantation. Either side were soldiers camped along the waterway waving and shouting to us, telling us we had come too late, with a few expletives thrown in. Whether we came too late or not I don't know. I know I was out there three and a half years after that.

At last we docked at Basra, and Army trucks were waiting to take us out to the camp and REME No 1 Base workshop, about 60 or 70 miles out on the Sheiba Desert. Having reckoned the number of hours we were sailing, at an average of about 13 knots, I thought we must have sailed about 20,000 miles from Scotland to Basra, which is a long way in U boat infested waters. Thanks to the Royal Navy we got through without incident.

**Winter, Iraq –
Syl and Tommy just had tea,
tin cup and plate in hand**

Chapter 5
Iraq

It was now March as we arrived on the Sheiba Desert in Iraq and the temperature was getting up to about anywhere from 115^0F to 123^0F in the shade. The workshops we had to work in were big hangars made of corrugated iron and I have seen the temperatures get as high as 135^0F inside them, it was like working in an oven.

Our camp huts had half round roofs like Nissan huts, and they were covered in straw then plastered over with mud and sand to keep the heat off, and the hut cooler from the sun. They had no windows, just wooden shutters covered in plaited straw, the same with the doors. There were about 34 men to a hut and we made our own beds with four pieces of wood for an oblong frame, four legs to keep it off the floor, then a piece of canvas nailed to the frame to form a mattress, all scrounged from our workshop. An empty wooden tea chest or box of some sort became a bedside cabinet to keep things in such as soap, toothpaste, and shaving tackle. An empty tin, which had supplied us with dehydrated potatoes, or some other dehydrated food, was cut down and became our wash tin and was used to wash our clothes in, very primitive but useful, and we kept these under our beds.

One incident I remember very well was when we had a new Regimental Officer, who had just come out from the UK. Whilst we were at work he had gone around the huts, I suppose to see if they were tidy, and he spotted the tins under every bed and must have thought we used them to urinate in at night, like the old "jerries" or "gazundas", as they used to call them back home. He ordered them to be collected and dumped somewhere and we returned from work to find no wash tins, so someone went to ask where they were, found out where they had been dumped and brought them back. The Regimental Officer was ridiculed by the whole of 23 Workshop Company; he was posted somewhere else about two weeks later so we got rid of him.

It's funny he didn't ask someone what they were for because about three or four yards outside the huts were desert lilies, as they were called. It was a purpose built urinal made like a big funnel, about two feet in diameter at the top, tapering down to a spout four feet long and three inches in diameter. A hole was dug in the sand to take about two feet of the spout and these were used to urinate in at night, the urine soaking into the desert. Of course, the new

Rain Iraq, Mud and straw roof leaking - Tommy in foreground, tarpaulin sheets to cover roof - Tommy Moat in the foreground.jpg

Tommy, in Iraq, 1944
going for water to wash and shave.

60

Winter, Iraq 1944 – Just off guard duty, Syl, Tommy and Doug.

Officer from the UK would never have seen anything like it and the desert lilies were a standing joke.

I remember one morning when we were getting ready for work parade, my mate Tommy, who was in the next bed to me, said that he was going on sick parade that morning. I asked him what the matter was and he said, 'I had to get up for a piss last night. I went outside to the piss tin, and don't know what happened, I must have fainted, because when I came to I was laid down at the side of it, so I'm going sick to find out if there is anything wrong with me.'

The Doctor saw him and thought he had only fainted, so sent him back to work. We all had a laugh at Tommy lying down with desert lily for the night. We had to make our own fun.

Chapter 6
Humour in Uniform

I should mention at this stage that Tommy had a very dry sense of humour. If he told us a joke it was always short and funny and one we could have told our mothers. Here are two of his staple jokes. He would start off by saying, 'Did I ever tell you the one about the load of monkeys?' Then he would start.

'There were these two men who passed each other as they went to work each morning and they just passed the time of day. However, this morning one man said to the other, cutting his words like we do in Lancashire, "Has ta seen a lorry load of monkeys going up yon?"

'The man replied, "Why, has ta fell off?"'

Of course, the funny part was that Tommy was always laughing before he got to the end, and we laughed because we had heard them so many times before.

His other joke was about the Sergeant Major inspecting the guard. 'He inspected them at the front then inspected them from the rear. He stopped at one soldier, tapped him on the shoulder and said, "Am I hurting you?"

'The soldier said, "No Sir."'

Left to right standing, name unknown, Dick Abram, Fred Cooper, and seated, Tommy Moat. Iraq 1944

'The Sergeant Major then said, "I should be, I'm standing on your hair, get a hair cut."

Tommy just roared laughing; we couldn't help but laugh having heard it so often. It was all good fun and broke the monotony of everyday life.

I remember another funny incident regarding Tommy. He had been on leave to Beirut in Lebanon. The man in charge of the leave party was Quartermaster Sergeant Fields. During the journey in trucks for three nights Tommy had struck up a kind of friendship with the Quartermaster because they both came from the Manchester area so had a lot in common to talk about. I remember Mr Fields wasn't all that popular with the rank and file, yet Tommy couldn't speak too highly of him and said what a grand fellow he was after being on leave with him. Of course, when anyone returns from leave, within a couple of days they are put on guard duty and Tommy was no exception to the rule. Now Tommy didn't like cleaning his rifle and equipment for guard duty and he wasn't quite as fussy as the rest of us and I remember him calling me a right bullshitter when going on guard duty, so I told him to remember what the army tells all new recruits, "it's bullshit but it looks nice – and bullshit baffles brains".

As it happened Quartermaster Sergeant Fields was the Orderly Officer for the day when Tommy was on guard, therefore he had to inspect the guard before they mounted. When Mr Fields came to Tommy he ordered him to Port Arms for inspection. Tommy obeyed thrusting his rifle forward to eye level, withdrawing the bolt and sticking his thumb in the bolthole so his thumbnail reflected light up the rifle barrel, whilst Mr Fields looked down it from the other end. Of course, Quartermaster Sergeant Fields would know Tommy, having been friendly with him on leave. As soon as he looked down the barrel Mr Fields turned to the guard commander and said, 'Take this man's name for having a dirty rifle on guard and put him on a charge.' So Tommy was for the high jump.

When Tommy came back to the hut to collect his blanket to take it down to the guardroom for the night he said to us lads, 'What do you think has happened? That blasted Quartermaster Sergeant Fields has put me on a charge for having a dirty rifle on guard.'

One of the lads said, 'I thought Fields was a pal of yours.'

'Not anymore,' Tommy replied.

Another lad said, 'That'll learn you for getting too friendly with Fields.' Mind you, his words were more coarse and explicative than mine.

Tommy ended up cleaning rifles for three nights in the armoury. It was quite a laugh for us, and a long time before Tommy lived it down saying what a grand chap Mr Fields was on leave.

Here is another story I thought I ought to relate which could be either funny or annoying, depending where you were at the time. Just as there is a rota in the army for guard duty, there is a rota for Orderly Officer for the day. He is on duty for 24 hours to see the regimental side runs according to orders, or to deal with any emergency, especially in the night. His day starts at 5 or 6am reveille and finishes at reveille the following day. He has to see all parades are carried out on time and that the cookhouse has the meals on time and properly cooked. He usually asks the men if they have any complaints about the food, which can be really funny. I have seen men stand up to complain and before they got their complaint out the Orderly Officer would shout 'Sit down,' and that is as far as he would get with the complaint, which was a big laugh as you can imagine.

He also has to inspect the guard when they go on and off duty, see the guardroom is organised and see that everyone knows their duty on each sentry post. He is also within his right to quietly approach a sentry at any time during the night and order him to turn out the guard. The sentry on the gate across from the guardroom would then shout out, 'Turn out the guard,' and within seconds the men in the guardroom are supposed to turn out ready for action, and this could happen at any time between shifts, often about 1am or 3am. Of course, when you come off your guard duty of two hours you then have four hours in the guardroom to lie down but not get undressed. You can take your steel helmet off, loosen your belt and webbing equipment and lie on the bed with your rifle alongside, so if the guard is called out you are ready instantly. I have been in the guardroom when called out, and I have been on sentry when ordered by the Orderly Officer to call out the guard say at 1am, which could be laughable. Some chaps came out with one boot on and trying to get the other on and it was really funny from where I was standing. When they did get out, the Orderly Officer would give them a right rollicking, then perhaps turn them out again half an hour later to keep them on their toes.

I think some of these Officers did it for a bit of fun and our Workshop Officer was no exception; his name was Captain Myles. He was a big chap, about 6 feet tall, broad shoulders, no fat on him, probably in his middle twenties, the same as us. He was quite good to get on with as Workshop Officer but knew nothing about our job, he just ran the shop allocating the work.

On this particular day Maurice Hellier and I were working together. Captain Myles came over to us and Maurice said, 'I see you are Orderly Officer today sir.'

'Yes, that's right Maurice, I'm on call for the next 24 hours,' he replied.

Now, Captain Myles was noted for turning the guard out at some unearthly hour and Maurice went on to say, 'You won't be turning the guard out tonight will you sir? Only Syl and I are on guard tonight.'

'Oh Maurice,' Captain Myles said, 'I wouldn't do a thing like that, especially now I know you and Syl are on guard.'

So at 6pm Maurice and I, along with others, paraded for guard inspection, inspected by Captain Myles, then marched off to the guardroom for a 12 hour shift, two hours on and four off. All went well until about 3am when the sentry on the gate shouted, 'Turn out the guard.' We all shuffled outside. Captain Myles had a word with us then ordered us back to the guardroom, most of us complaining under our breath.

The following day when the guard had dismounted at 6am we had breakfast then paraded for work, no time off for having been on guard all night. During the morning Captain Myles came over to Maurice and me in the workshop and Maurice said to him, 'I thought you said yesterday you wouldn't turn the guard out last night knowing Syl and I were on guard!'

Captain Myles replied, 'Oh, I forgot you two were on guard, of course I have to keep you young lads on your toes,' and he walked away, laughing. That's how he was, it was just a bit of fun to him at 3am, yet he was a likeable sort of fellow.

He came from Southend or Southsea. I understood his father had those little motorboats you could hire out for an hour or so, and I could imagine Captain Myles after the war with his megaphone shouting to some of these pleasure boats, 'Time's up, come in number 15, come in number 12,' and so on. It takes all sorts to form an army in wartime.

Of course, when you have worked all day then go straight on guard for 12 hours and you try to get a bit of rest between shifts, then someone shouts "turn out the guard" at 1am for no good reason, it can be quite annoying, but that's soldiering, you just get on with your duty.

I recollect the following, which always brings a laugh when recounted. We were still in Iraq, but the war had moved into Italy and Germany and demob was still a long way off. However, someone in the top brass decided to give all us chaps a form for us to state whether we liked the trade we had chosen as apprentices, or if we would like to train for some other trade after the war.

I was quite happy with my trade having been an apprentice motor bodybuilder. All motor bodies were built in ash timber in those days. It was interesting work, everything being shaped in curves, yet I would have liked to have been able to build railway carriages, so I put that on my form. Others wanted to change to bricklayers or perhaps sign writers.

As always amongst a cross section of men, you always get a joker. Life wouldn't be the same without them and this is where the laugh comes in. One lad wrote on the form that he wanted to change his trade and be trained as a brothel keeper! We all had a good laugh at that. I dare say the top brass who went through the forms had a good laugh too. We never ever heard what happened to the forms so I suppose the project was abandoned with request to be trained as brothel keepers!

This is another incident that went on with a young Iraqi and Tommy. The Iraqis around us I would think, were quite poor, and for some reason Tommy didn't like them In fact they were still living like Abraham and Isaac in biblical times. Apart from growing a few date palms irrigated near the banks of the Tigris or Euphrates rivers, there didn't seem to be much else going on.

We were on the Sheiba desert, the nearest little town called Asher was about 30 miles away. Many Arabs were employed by the British Government as labourers in our Army Workshops; what they were paid I don't know. The currency out there was in Fills, a 1,000 Fills to a Deana, which was a pound-note equivalent to our pound sterling. We had 240 pence to the pound in those days as against 1,000 Iraqi Fills to a Deana, so a Fill was valued at less than a farthing in sterling. Even if you had 125 Fills it was only worth half a crown, two shillings and sixpence.

To get back to my story, there was a soldier in our 23 Workshop Company who had been a barber as a civilian, so he came round after work doing haircuts, he charged 6 pence, about 25 Fills. I remember his name was Cross, and he came from Norfolk. Sometimes in the evening, or on a Sunday, a young Iraqi barber would come to the camp and go round the huts doing haircuts. When he had cut your hair we asked him how much? He would reply, 'As you like Johnny, as you like.' Some chaps would give him 15 Fills or 20 Fills, which was less than Cross charged, so we were a few Fills better off.

Now Tommy didn't like this Iraqi saying, "As you like Johnny, as you like." Tommy said it makes it sound as if he's well off. He said, 'Next time he cuts my hair I'll surprise him.' So when he cut Tommy's hair again Tommy said, 'How much?'

He replied, 'As you like Johnny, as you like.' So Tommy got his leather purse out, fiddled inside, pulled out 2 Fills and put it in the Iraqi's hand. The Iraqi, obviously shocked, held out his hand for more saying, 'This no good Johnny, no good.'

Tommy said, 'You said "as you like, as you like", that's as I like, 2 Fills.'

'No, no Johnny, this not enough.' So Tommy then fiddled in his purse, pulled out another one Fill, and put it in his hand, which was like adding insult to injury. The Iraqi then said, 'Me no cut hair for you,' and he never did.

We then told Tommy what a tight fisted devil he was. All he did was have a good laugh and said it was "as I liked", but Tommy always had to pay 25 fills to Cross for a haircut after that because he had given the Iraqi less than 3 farthings for his haircut. Tommy thought it funny, but he ended up out of pocket with his joke.

This is another funny story that happened to a chap in our company. The Officers in charge of a company of 400 men would consist of about 4 Lieutenants, 2 Captains and a Major Company Commander. Anything above Major, say Lieutenant Colonel or Colonel would be in HQ Company, so we fellows seldom saw these high rank officers.

Anyway, it seems that one of these Colonels had suggested to his colleagues that it would be an idea to build an old fashioned fireplace in their mess to remind them of home. It seems the Colonel with the idea was Colonel Saddler. The next thing was to find a brick setter amongst the ranks, and in order to do this all the other rank pay books were called into the company office to find anyone who had been a brick setter as a civilian. Even though our outfit was electrical, mechanical engineers, they weren't all skilled tradesmen, some were army trained, and we skilled men kept them right. You see, a man who was a skilled tailor in civvy street would be a textile worker, repairing tents or lorry canopies. We had a painter painting lorries whom as a civilian was a highly skilled Church Painter and Sign Writer.

What the selected brick setter did in the army, was to change tyres on lorries. In any case, he was told by the Company Sergeant Major to build a fireplace in the Officers' Mess, as required, and that Colonel Saddler had volunteered to labour for him, mixing mortar and carrying bricks.

We were all supplied with overalls like boiler suits, the tops and trousers all in one piece, to work in, and the brick setter arrived at the Officers' Mess with trowel and level in his overalls too. There was a pile of bricks there with sand and cement, but no Colonel Saddler. However, after a short time a little fellow turned up in overalls telling the brick setter he had been sent to labour for him and he had a drawing of the fireplace to be built for him. So the brick setter told this chap how to mix the mortar and to get some bricks carried in because it didn't look as though this so and so Saddler was coming. So with a lot of F***ing and cursing about Saddler the brick setter got to work.

They stopped for a rest mid morning whilst the labourer brought some tea from the mess, and by dinnertime Colonel Saddler had still not turned up. They got working again with the brick setter cursing about Saddler having the idea to build a fireplace then leaving it to the other ranks to get on with it.

Anyway, they built the fireplace, and as they swept up with the brick setter still F***ing and cursing about Saddler the labourer said, 'The fireplace looks well.'

The brick setter said, 'Will that so and so Saddler like it?'

The labourer said, 'I think so, because I am Colonel Saddler and I've had a real entertaining day.'

What a laugh they both had, with the brick setter cursing Saddler all day not knowing Saddler was the labourer with the overalls on.

In our section of the hut were three men from Yorkshire, three from Lancashire, one from Lincoln and one from London, so as you can imagine we had some fierce arguments about Lancashire and Yorkshire, but we were all good mates working and doing guard duty together.

On this particular night the lads from Lancashire were giving their opinions as to why it was better than Yorkshire. We had the second largest docklands in the world at Liverpool, a marvellous piece of engineering with Blackpool Tower, and the finest dance venue, the Tower Ballroom, with music supplied by the Mighty Wurlitzer Organ. One of the Yorkshire men then said that we had nobody in Lancashire who could play the Wurlitzer so they had sent Reginald Dixon to play it. That caused a big laugh, but was true, as he came from Sheffield.

Chapter 7
Further Snapshots of Iraq

The base workshops and camps were seven miles around the perimeter. There were about twelve hundred REME tradesmen and there were RAOC men with stores and hundred of Indian troops, mainly Ghurkhas. We repaired and maintained anything that moved - trucks, staff cars, motorcycles, bicycles, tanks, Bren gun carriers, guns, rifles, and machine guns. The reason for us being in Iraq was to occupy the country because of the oil wells.

The worst thing about Iraq was the extreme heat, even at night. Everything was so hot it never got below $80\text{-}85^0\text{F}$ at night from March to October and even in the winter months it was always around $80\text{-}90^0\text{F}$ in daytime. We were supposed to drink at least 13 pints of water a day. Everyone carried a Chagall full of water with them, it was made of canvas and allowed the water to seep out slowly so the water inside was always cold. The more you drank the more you perspired, and the more you perspired the more you drank. If you stopped perspiring and drinking, within hours you were down with heat exhaustion. The reason we were able to stand the high temperature was the low humidity, a dry heat. Usually about October the humidity rose for about

Left to right – Bahon Ram, Sylvester Till and Joga Ram.

Sylvester Till and Ramachandran
Iraq 1944

Back row - Bignall, Maurice Hellier, Tommy Moat. Front row - two Gurkhas, George Atkinson one Punjabi Soldier. Iraq 1944.

No.1 Base workshop R.E.M.E Football Team 1943-44 Iraq.
Front row second left Jimmy Blevins, A Scot centre forward. next to him
Colonel Bonalack, Commanding Officer, next Andy Campbell, Captain.

Iraq
Washing Sunday morning. Doug, Syl and Tommy.

two weeks, which really sapped our energy. The Arabs said if they didn't get those two weeks of high humidity the dates on the date palms didn't ripen, so there was a reason for it.

Nearly all our entertainment was drawn from talent amongst the men who formed a concert party about twice a year, usually at Christmas time. There were men who could play piano or violin, it was usually the Scotsmen who played the violin, and there were accordion players, saxophonists, trumpeters, drummers and mouth organists, they were all quite good too. We also had singers who were very good too. The Regimental Sergeant Major always sang, *"I'll take you home again Kathleen"*, Jimmy Blevins, a Scots lad from Stirling always sang *"Bonny Mary of Argyle"* and *"I Love a Lassie"*. Another lad sang *"Roses of Picardy"*, all very good songs.

I think that we only had two ENSA Concert Parties visit us in the whole two and a half years I was there, one was from Wales and the other from South Africa. They were white South Africans and one girl sang a South African song called *"Take me back to the old Transvaal"*. You could tell as she sang it that she was thinking about her homeland. Another song was one of Deanna Durbin's, which was popular at that time, called *"Spring will be a Little Late This Year"*. All these things stick in one's memory.

There were also sad things to remember. As I mentioned earlier, our comrade who was known as Rommel, who jumped off the bus in Manchester as he went on embarkation leave to see his young wife and two little girls, became a despatch rider on a motorbike for our company in Iraq. He was on his way with some despatches and had an accident out in the desert. I don't know what happened but he was killed, and I have often thought what sad news it would have been for his young wife and two little girls. There wouldn't be any victory celebrations for them when the war finished. Sadly, we lost about four men due to accidents.

Another incident I am not likely to forget occurred on the second Christmas in Iraq. Anyone who has been in the army knows there are two types of orders, which you must familiarise yourself with. Daily orders, which go on the notice board every day and which everyone must read, which comprise names for guard duty or fire picket, who is going on leave, or some place you may have to report to at a certain time. Then there are Standing Orders, usually near the camp entrance, stating what you must not do whilst in that camp. Once you have read them you should remember them and if you break them you are in trouble. I had been in the camp for nearly two years and by that time had forgotten them, however, that was no excuse if you did break them.

This was Christmas and I had a little Ensign box camera. I managed to get a 120 film for it, and along with my two mates, Tommy from Ashton-U-Lime and Dennis from Dalton-In-Furness. We decided that on our Christmas Day off we would take photographs of the lads and huts, etc. We had two photographs left on the film and decided to finish it by taking photographs of a German mobile gun captured at El Aliment, I think it had been brought to us to boost morale. So we walked out to the gun in the desert, within the perimeter of the base and I sat on it with Tommy whilst Dennis took a photograph. Then Dennis sat on the gun and Tommy took the photograph showing the big black cross on the turret, like Germans had on their aeroplane wings. We thought the photograph would make a nice souvenir.

To get the film developed I sent it with one of our chaps who went down with various documents to a little place called Asher, about thirty miles away, a place about as big as Kirkham, in order that it could be developed by an Arab photographer. He left the film and collected it the following

Monday. It seems that during the week a Security Officer from Baghdad had been to check on the Arab photographer and found my film with the German mobile gun on it. He confiscated it, took it back to Baghdad and then sent it back to my Company Commanding Officer, stating that Standing Orders had been broken by me, having photographed an enemy vehicle. I was charged with breaking Standing Orders and had to report to the Company Sergeant Major to be brought before Commanding Officer Captain Williams Green.

I was marched in and the Captain showed me the photograph. It was perfect. He asked me if I had anything to say in my defence, but what could I saw with a photograph as proof? I said, 'Sir, it was just a bit of fun on Christmas Day, I had no intention of breaching any security.'

He replied, 'Unfortunately this has come from GHQ Baghdad, and Standing Orders have been broken, and I can't deal with it, so I'll adjourn the case to Base Headquarters for 4 o'clock tomorrow.' This was like going from the Magistrate's Court to the Sessions Court where they could give me more punishment, so I wasn't feeling too good about this knowing that Captain Williams Green could give be seven days CB (confined to barracks).

The following day I reported to Base Headquarters and waited for the Regimental Sergeant Major, a very smart regular soldier. His name was RSM Dean, known amongst the lads as Dixie Dean (as long as he never heard you say it). RSM's are untouchable, they run the whole show and even though I had been in the base for nearly two years I had never met him, only at a distance on parade ground where he was Lord. However, at 4pm he came marching up with his stick under his arm.

He came to me and asked if I was Craftsman Till. I sprang smartly to attention and answered, 'Yes Sir.'

He then said, 'Stand at ease;' then went on to say, 'Colonel Sadler is trying you and two other Officers, I will go in and see if they are ready for you.'

He came out and asked me if I knew what the procedure was. I replied 'No Sir.'

He went on to say, 'I will march you in. Colonel Sadler will read the charge out and ask you if you have anything to say in defence. I will then march you out again whilst they decide what to do with you.'

I was marched in, the charge was read out, "Breaking Standing Orders by photographing an enemy vehicle", did I have anything to say?

I said I had no intention of breaking any security, it was just a bit of fun on Christmas Day. I said I was not guilty really because I was on both photographs so I could not have taken them as charged.

Colonel Sadler then said, 'Will you give us the names of the men who took the photographs?'

I said, 'I can't do that Sir, they are my mates and the camera was mine, also the film, and I sent it down to Asher to be developed.'

He then said, 'You are not really guilty, but you are an accessory to the charge and we can't let you off. We have to send a report back to Baghdad.'

With that the RSM marched me out and had a chat with me outside. He said he had spoken to my Company Commanding Officer and Company Sergeant Major who both gave me a good report and said they had never had any trouble with me. He had spoken to my Workshop Officer who also said there were no problems. He went on to say that he too, had seen me about the base and had had no trouble with me, so he said he would go in with these reports and do his best for me.

The RSM then came out and marched me in again. I had to take my hat off whilst Colonel Sadler read the sentence: "14 days confined to barracks"

The RSM then marched me out, told me I would have to parade with defaulters at 6pm with guard every night. When the guard had been marched off I had to get back to my hut, change into my overalls and report to the Orderly Officer for the day. He would then tell me where to report for jinkers or fatigues.

RSM Dean then said, 'Laddie, if you ever have need to develop a film again bring it to me, I can get it done for you for nothing in the Base.' He then went on to say, 'It seems most unfair because I know there isn't an Officer or senior NCO that hasn't got a photo of that German mobile gun, but unfortunately you were caught.' He then shook hands with me. I had a great respect for RSM Dean, he was strict but fair, and no doubt he will be on the great parade ground in the sky by now. The funny part was after I had paraded with defaulters and the guard had been marched down to the guardroom I could never find the Orderly Officer to tell me where to report for fatigues, so I never had any fatigues to do. I feel sure RSM Dean had arranged that with the Officers. At 9pm when my fatigues were supposed to finish

I had to sign in at the guardroom every half hour until lights out at 10.30pm to prove I was in camp. At 6am reveille I had to report to the guardroom within ten minutes to prove I had been in camp all night. Where else could I have been with only hundreds of miles of desert outside the base? Nevertheless it was a long day from 6am to 10.30pm, particularly as I had been in the workshop all day. I felt the worst part was parading with defaulters alongside the guard. On the first three nights there were two other defaulters with me, one for needing a haircut on guard duty, the other for having a dirty rifle on guard. For the next eleven nights I was on my own. I felt like a real criminal and of course, all the guards from our company knew I wasn't the type to be in trouble.

I will never forget the last defaulters' parade I came off. I was going back to the hut to change when one of the Yorkshire lads named Bill Curry, who was in our section of the hut was coming back from the transport compound and he caught me up. He said, 'Have you finished tonight Syl?' I replied that I had. He then said, 'Just hold back a bit whilst I go ahead and get the lads to give you a big hand.' He went ahead and as I approached the hut all the shutters went up, then there were cheers and clapping and shouts of "Good old Tilly". So that was quite a nice end to my 14 days CB.

During my stay in Iraq we never seemed to be short of water, yet it only rained one week a year at about the end of January. Of course it was always cold water for washing clothes. These dried in about an hour and were ready to wear again. We had to shave, wash and shower in cold water with no privacy at all. We got seven days leave every six months and went to Baghdad, which was about 150 miles away. The trains all had wooden seats with no proper toilets, just a cubicle with a hole in the floor and we always had to travel at night.

Baghdad wasn't as magical as one is led to believe. We always stayed at the YMCA and were taken out on trips in the city and shown around various Mosques. On some afternoons there were lectures about Iraq. The heat was as bad there as back at the base workshops and Baghdad is in the desert too. It was just a change from work and duties. Halfway between our base and Baghdad was a railway junction called Ur Junction. Ur is mentioned in the Old Testament of *The Bible*, so it was all very historical.

After we had been in Iraq for about a year, a leave camp was opened up in Lebanon, right on the edge of the

Mediterranean Sea. I went twice but it was about 900 miles from our base in Iraq. We got the train overnight to Baghdad, then spent the following day in a transit camp. Trucks filled with bags of sand to weigh them down were laid on for us to travel all night to the next transit camp, as it was too hot to travel in the daytime. We rested in camp the following day then set off again in the trucks to the next transit camp at night. There were no proper roads, just tracks across the desert. We rested again the following day and set off again at night into Syria. Our next stop was Damascus. We stayed there all day and all night and set off in daylight on our last stretch into Lebanon and Beirut. Of course Damascus is mentioned in *The Bible* where it states that a blinding light from heaven struck down Saul, as he came near Damascus so he couldn't see. He was told by God to go to Damascus to the street called Straight, which is still there. I have walked along it. Saul stayed in a house in this street and God sent a prophet, Ananias to see Saul and to restore his sight. His name was changed to Paul and he followed the Lord. So I have seen quite a lot whilst soldiering.

**Street called Straight, Damascus
Syria 1945.**

After leaving Damascus, which is mainly desert, we travelled in daylight into Lebanon which is very hilly with a lot of hairpin bends as it drops down to the leave camp in Beirut, with the lovely Mediterranean Sea to swim in outside the tents. Everything was much greener with lovely trees. The temperature was about 80 or 90^0F, which was quite mild to us. It was so nice to get away from sandstorms, which blew up for weeks, and to get into the nice clean air and sea.

In the leave camp we could get up anytime, there was no regimentation at all. Breakfast was served from 7 to 9am, dinner was 12 to 2pm and tea from 4 to 6pm. There were trips organised by the army to historical places such as the ruins of Balbeck, etc. We had seven days leave in Beirut then we had to make the journey back to base in Iraq by truck and train at night. It was a long trip but worth it. I did the trip twice and I remember as we arrived in Damascus the second time, on our way back the headlines in the newspaper were "War finished in Europe". It was 4th May 1945, VE Day was 8th May. It was welcome news, but Japan hadn't given up and we were wondering whether we would get sent further East, because troops were not supposed to serve in Iraq more than 18 months - two years at the outside. I had been there for two years at that time and I suppose as the war had moved into Italy and Germany, the troops which should have replaced us never arrived, so we had to stay on.

In about June 1945, not long after I had been on leave to Beirut, some regimental type decided that 23 Workshop Company ought to have some regimental training, so it was decided by the top brass that the whole company should be sent out on the Sheiba desert on manoeuvres. Of course this had to be done in our own time, not workshop time.

The whole company was split into four sections consisting of one section with about 200 men, the other three sections with about 60 or 70 men in each. The 200 men were taken in trucks out to a location on the desert to defend it. The other three sections were to march out in different directions from the base in order to surround the desert defence post, attack and capture it.

We set off, marching from base on the Saturday night at about 7pm. We had a Lieutenant and some senior NCO's in charge, and of course planning the route to this defence location in the desert is like being at sea, there are no landmarks, your position has to be worked out by speed and compass direction. Troops reckon to march about four miles an hour, stopping every two hours for fifteen minutes. The Lieutenant marched us until about 1am, so allowing for fifteen minute breaks we must have been about twenty miles out on the desert to a certain compass position. We were then told to try to get some sleep by just lying down on the desert using our packs as pillows. Reveille would be at 4am.

So after three hour's rest we started marching again in order to rendezvous with the other two sections and attack the defence post at 5am. Of course it was daylight and there was no sign of any men or trucks in the defence position. So the Lieutenant marched us on until after 9am and there were still no signs of any defence post. He marched us on until nearly 10am. By this time he must have formed the opinion that he was lost, and the day was getting hotter, we had only one bottle of water each, which was running low as we had to drink more. We were now five hours overdue our compass location and it wouldn't be long before we started to dehydrate, so he decided to call a halt. He didn't know where he was in the desert so he wouldn't be able to retrace his steps, and none of us were in a fit state to march any further. The only protection we had against the sun was our thick straw topees and we had no water supply. Things were looking serious.

Twelve o'clock midday came and went, we were lost and hoping some of the other troops would find us. It got to two thirty and some of the older men, in their thirties and forties were becoming exhausted. Then we heard a motorbike. We stood up and thankfully he saw us and came riding across. He had several chagils of water tied to his motorbike so the chaps who were in a bad way got a drink, then off he went to direct trucks to our position, along with two or three ambulances. They put the worst chaps in the ambulances and the rest of us were piled into the trucks.

We were taken back to camp and after plenty of water we soon recovered and had breakfast at teatime. The whole exercise had been a disaster and could have ended up far worse if it hadn't been for the despatch rider.

It wasn't long after this disaster that I started to feel the exhaustion of being in Iraq for two years. My heart kept missing a beat when I lay down at night so I reported sick. Our Medical Officer was Polish and he didn't like the English. He said there was nothing wrong with me and sent me back to work, so of course I became more and more exhausted. I reported sick again and asked to see a specialist, then I was sent to the 61st British General Hospital about three miles away. The specialist was a

Colonel in the Medical Corps. He gave me a thorough examination and then asked me how long I had been in Iraq. I told him two and a half years. He said that I must be sent out of the country immediately and told me he would give me a letter to give to my Medical Officer. A week later I was posted to Tel El Kebir in Egypt. I was certainly glad to get away from Iraq.

Chapter 8
On to Egypt

So for the last time I boarded the train with wooden seats on the Sheiba Desert to travel overnight to Baghdad, arriving about 8am. We went in a transit camp for the day to rest ready for our journey across the desert to Damascus. The transport this time wasn't army trucks, it was two coaches run by a firm called Nairns Transport. I think it was a Scots firm who specialised in this run from Baghdad to Damascus and back. They didn't take the army route but blazed a trail straight across the desert on the old camel route. I remember we boarded the coaches with our iron rations for the journey about 7pm. The first coach was quite big and new, but I was in the second older coach following on behind. The army trucks took three nights to do the trip but these coaches blazing a straight trail left Baghdad at 7pm and reckoned to be in Damascus by 12 o'clock noon the following day, allowing for ten or fifteen minute rests. This would amount to about 16 hours and reckoning an average speed of about 35 miles an hour the distance must have been about 560 miles, quite a long way.

Everything went well with us until dawn the following day when our coach just came to a stop. The front coach

Broken Down - leaving Iraq 1945.

went blazing on, not knowing we had broken down. He wouldn't be able to see much behind with all the dusty sand he churned up. However, about an hour later he came back to look for us. On examination of our coach they found the drive shaft to the back axle had broken off, so even though the engine ran there was no drive to the wheels. A rope was got out and the front coach took us in tow.

After a long dirty dusty journey we arrived in Damascus about 5pm, five hours overdue, although after a good wash and shave we were none the worse for the experience. We then went on to a transit camp for about two days to await a train from Damascus into Palestine as it was then, then into Egypt to Tel El Kebir, number 2 base workshops.

This was a massive military base with a 20 mile perimeter, there were tank regiments, infantry regiments, Medical Corps, Royal Corps of Signals, Service Corps, Royal Engineers, Ordnance Corps, and my regiment, REME. In fact it was the Aldershot of the Middle East. I was put in L Camp.

Whenever I was posted to a new camp it always took time for the men to get accustomed to my names and this amusing little incident happened when I arrived in Tel El Kebir. I reported to the camp company office, which was just a tent. I told the Sergeant who was sitting on a stool at a table that I had been posted to L camp.

'Right,' he said, 'name, rank and number?'

I replied, 'Till.'

He said, 'It's your name I want.'

I said, 'Till is my name.'

He wrote it down and I was thinking about what he would think about my Christian name if he thought Till was a bit odd.

'Christian name?' he shouted.

'Sylvester spelled with a Y,' I said.

He whipped round on his stool and shouted in a real northern accent, 'Are you trying to take the piss out of me?'

'No Sergeant,' I replied, 'that's my name.'

He then said, 'What are you, a bloody film star or something? Give me your pay book.'

Now a soldier's pay book is his identity, it contains his whole army history, name, rank, number, call up date, leave dates, inoculations, etc, date of overseas embarkation leave, promotions, everything until demob date. I gave the Sergeant my pay book to prove my name and he started to thumb through it.

After a few minutes he turned to me with a different attitude altogether and said, 'I see by your embarkation leave date that you have been abroad over three and a half years.'

I said, 'That's correct Sergeant.'

He then said, 'I thought I had been out here a long time, nearly two years.'

I then said, 'It's like this Sergeant, I've been in Iraq before coming here and you've probably heard what sort of place that is. As you can see by my pay book I may have a fancy name but I have too much service in to try taking the mick out of Sergeants! But you must admit you are talking to an old campaigner now, as proved by my pay book. The Sergeant was much more polite after that little encounter.

I hadn't been there many days when I realised it was far better than being on the Sheiba Desert in Iraq. The temperature didn't get to more than about 80 or 85^0F, which was quite mild to me, and it cooled off at night so you could sleep better. We were housed in quite big tents, eight to a tent, and the food was much better. All our food in Iraq was dehydrated. There were two cinemas, a theatre, a lovely outdoor swimming pool, the walls around the pool had been decorated by Italian prisoners with bathing belles, some nude. We could get refreshments too and the canteens were good. We could get egg and chips, sausage and chips, ice cream, fruit etc., None of this was ever in Iraq. I came to the conclusion I was going to like being there.

About July 1945, I was due for another leave and went for seven days to a leave camp at Nathania in Palestine as it was then. Some days the army ran trucks fitted with seats to places like Jerusalem, Bethlehem and the Dead Sea, which is so salty it is impossible to sink, you just float, quite an experience. I went to the Sea of Galilee and the River Jordan, all very interesting having read about them in *The Bible* where Jesus and his disciples had been. When I read about these places as a young lad I never imagined I would visit them.

My leave ended and I had to wend my way back by train to Tel El Kebir and work and duties, however, it wasn't long after on the 15th September 1945 that the Japanese surrendered so the World War had finished, but demob was still a long way off.

One day when we came back from workshops, there was a new chap in our tent. His name was Wilkinson known as Wilky. He was about six feet tall, a likeable fellow with a Liverpool accent. He had an army push bike, which he leaned against the tent pole. He was a joiner and had been at Tel Kebir a long time. He never came to our workshops, he said he was on maintenance work around the base. We never saw him on any parades except for pay parade - he always turned up for that.

Each morning when we went on workshop parade, Wilky cleared off on the bike somewhere. He eventually told us that he had nicked the bike from outside some army officers quarters in the base. No doubt it would be a Sergeant Major's bike – they had them to ride around on and with a base as big as Tel El Kebir, twenty miles round, they would need one, so some Sergeant Major would be minus a bike.

Wilky used the bike for other purposes. He told us that he had got friendly with the Manageress of one of the NAFFIs. When we went on work parade, Wilky got on his bike to go to the NAFFI were it seems he was sleeping with the Manageress who was in her forties. Wilky would be in his mid twenties, the same as us, so he was onto a good thing! No parades except for pay, the rest of the time he spent in bed with the Manageress.

How he got away with it, I really don't know, but with a place as big as Tel El Kebir it was easy to disappear if you had the nerve to do it.

Sadly, it seems Wilky wasn't satisfied with the good thing he was on with the Manageress. He got friendly with a NAFFI girl and the Manageress rumbled it and cleared Wilky out - which is how he ended up with a bike in our tent. He still cleared off every day, no doubt to sleep with the NAFFI girl, so there must have been something good about him.

He carried on this game every day until he was due to go back to U.K for demob. I remember as he left us on his last day, he shook hands with us and said "I'll leave you the bike lads, it may come in handy if you get friendly with the NAFFI manageress". I came home on demob a few weeks later, and the bike was still in the tent, leaning against the tent pole. No doubt it could tell a tale or two about Wilky's adventures on maintenance work!

The Egyptian Mail
"It's All Over"

Chapter 9
On Leave to Old Blighty

About this time a regulation came into force whereby anyone in the Middle East who had been out there for three and a half years was granted one month's leave back to the United Kingdom. I had over three and a half year's service so I qualified. The time was calculated from when we left the UK, which was in 1942. Within a few weeks my name went up on daily orders for me to get my kit ready to leave Tel El Kebir at about the end of October 1945.

I had to get the train up to Port Said at the entrance to the Suez Canal. When I got to Port Said a troopship was moored to a makeshift jetty in the estuary. I couldn't believe my eyes when I saw her name, it was the *Britannic* which I had sailed on from the Clyde to Durban in 1942. It was like meeting an old friend, and to think whilst I had been out there all that time she had been sailing amongst U boat infested waters and there she was, waiting to take me home for Christmas 1945.

*(I feel I ought to give a few details and history of the Britannic (III) having sailed so far on her during the war and have dedicated **Appendix I** of this book to a full description of her. I never saw or sailed on her again.)*

Of course there were thousands of other troops going on leave, some on demob, but there were nowhere near the number of men on her as there were when we left the Clyde in 1942.

So we left Port Said about the end of October. When in the Mediterranean Sea we called at Valletta Harbour in Malta to take a few more troops on board. We then sailed on through the Straits of Gibraltar and into the Atlantic Ocean, the Bay of Biscay and then the Irish Sea. I remember it was early on Saturday morning on the 1st December 1945 when we stood off Liverpool waiting for the tide to take us over the bar to dock at Princes Landing Stage, on the Mersey at Liverpool.

A military band was playing to welcome us home, along with refreshments provided by the Salvation Army and the Women's Voluntary Service, cups of tea and rock buns. Corporation buses were laid on to take us to Garston transit camp to get all our documentation, such as travel warrants, ration books and railway tickets. There were buses to take us back to Liverpool to catch our trains to different parts of the country, the men who had to travel furthest got away first. I got a train to Preston at approximately 4 p.m., arriving at Preston to catch the 6 p.m. bus to Freckleton and home. How wonderful it seemed to be home for a month, including Christmas.

Even though it was winter, it was nice to get into a nice bed at night with no reveille and no guard duty, just to be able to do as I liked, and yet my father still insisted that I had to be in by a certain time at night before the pubs closed! How silly, as I had been in the army for 5 years by then and he had no idea what I might have been up to, but there it was, I had to keep to the rules whilst I was under his roof!

Anyway, I had a very nice month to visit friends and relatives, but sadly all good things come to an end and the month just flew by. On New Year's Eve I had to get the bus and train back to the transit camp at Garston in Liverpool, and I remember it was freezing weather. Of course I knew I was to go back to Tel El Kebir, Egypt, but didn't know by what route or type of transport. The following morning, on New Year's Day in 1946, we boarded a train at Liverpool not knowing where we were heading for.

As the train steamed along through the frosty snow covered countryside, we realised by the station names that we were going south, and at about 5pm, as dusk fell, we drew into a siding, situated in an army camp. We got off the train for a meal and to bed down for the night in the huts. Reveille came, we went for breakfast then boarded the train waiting in the camp siding with steam up. We set off again through the snow-covered landscape and at about noon, steamed onto the dock at Newhaven in Sussex. We left the train to embark on a cross channel ferry to Dieppe in France where we had dinner in a camp then boarded a train for two nights and two days, taking us from Northern France to Toulon in Southern France; that was a long train journey. We entered another transit camp, and three days later boarded a troopship, which I never knew the name of, but I think it was American built. It was quite modern with bunk beds. No hammocks or sleeping on the deck.

We then set sail from Toulon and sailed down the Tyrrhenian Sea where we could see the masts of the French Navy ships showing above the sea where they had been scuttled to avoid capture by the Germans in the harbour. We sailed past Corsica, Sardinia and Sicily, into the Mediterranean Sea and past Malta to dock at Port Said in Egypt. This was February 1946. We then caught a train to Tel El Kebir and were back at number two base workshop to start vehicle repairs again.

Now I don't know if I was the only one from Freckleton who went overseas twice after being out in the Middle East for over three and a half years, then to travel out to the Middle East again. Little did I think when I went out in 1942 that I would go out again in 1946. I have never heard of anyone else doing it, it was quite an experience.

Chapter 10
Terrorists

When I got back to L Camp I found I had been promoted to a Full Corporal, two stripes. My pay went up and when I got demobbed my gratuity went up. I knew by then my demob number was for August 1946. With my two stripes, proficiency and overseas pay, my wages went up to eleven shillings a day, £3.17s. 0d a week. I was fed and clothed, plus seven days paid leave every three months, which wasn't bad compared with a tradesman in England who was on about two shillings an hour. A forty-six and a half-hour week came to £4.13s 0d, and they had to feed and clothe themselves, plus the expense of travelling to work.

Whilst I had been away, there were four new faces in the tent, all sent out from the UK, they hadn't been in the army long. Another man had been posted to us from Iraq, his name was Maurice and I had known him for a long time. He was one of the original 23 Workshop Company which had sailed on the *Britannic* from the Clyde in 1942, so it was nice to see him again. He had also been on a month's leave from Iraq to the UK and back and came from a little village called Henfield in Sussex, about twelve miles from Brighton.

One evening I remarked to the new young lads as they were writing letters home every other day, that when they had been out here as long as Maurice and me then they wouldn't have much to write about. They said that they were writing to their girlfriends and that if I had a girlfriend I'd have plenty to write about.

One of the lads said, 'The Corporal wouldn't write if he knew a girl.'

I replied, 'I would, but all the girls in my age group back home are married by now.'

Then Maurice handed me a slip of paper saying, 'Here is a girl you can write to, Syl.' When I looked at it he had given me his sister's name and address. I remember a few months before in Iraq, he had told me she was getting married, her name was Trixie.

I said, 'I am not writing to Trixie, she's married,' but Maurice then said that the wedding had not gone ahead.

Of course all the lads then dared me to write to her, so what could I do in front of all of them? So I got pen and paper and wrote to her explaining what had happened and I gave it to Maurice to post. The mail at that time was very good and within about five days I had a reply from Trixie. It was a very nice letter, she understood what had happened and sent me a photograph of herself. I had some snaps we had taken out there so I sent her one too. After that she invited me to go and see her after demob. I replied saying there were two places where I might be demobbed, one was Catterick in Yorkshire and the other Aldershot. If I got demobbed at Aldershot I would go down to see her whilst I was down that way, it would be in August sometime.

In the meantime both Maurice and I were due for another leave at the beginning of July in 1946. As it would be our last leave, we decided to go to Cyprus. We were given 14 days, allowing for travel by train and boat, little knowing the trouble we were heading for.

We boarded the train at Tel El Kebir and travelled up towards the mouth of the Suez Canal and crossed over the Quintana Bridge into Palestine. At that time they were forming the state of Israel by taking Palestinian land. The Palestinians were against this and terrorists began to operate. That was in 1946, and things have never been right since. On the day prior to our journey, the terrorists had stopped a train and turned everyone off and then set fire to it.

Anyway, we got into Palestine travelling through the night. The train was mainly full of troops, with a few

**In Cyprus on leave from Egypt 1946
Sylvester Till Age 27.**

Back row centre - Ted Bright, back row right, - Sylvester Till
Front row right Frank Warner
Egypt.

civilians on board. Most of us were trying to sleep, either on the floor or on the seats or luggage rack. I was on a luggage rack and Maurice was on the seat looking after our packs when the train slowed down to a snail speed. You could tell it was going very slowly by the long time it took to hear the clicks as the wheels went over the rail joints.

Then out of the quiet someone shouted that kit was being thrown off the train. There was quite a commotion as everyone started checking their kit. I jumped down to find my pack had gone, full of shirts, vests, underpants, socks, towels, soap, shaving things, scissors, brush, comb etc. I had nothing left except what I stood up in. It appeared that terrorists had slowed the train down to a crawl whilst they boarded and whilst we were sleeping they had thrown some of the kit off at the end of the corridor then jumped off. There were Military Police on the train so they came to take names and addresses of men and asked what kit they had lost. No one slept after that, and there I was going on leave to Cyprus without a change of clothes or anything to wash or shave with.

About noon the following day we arrived at the Palestine Port of Haifa to board an old wreck of a ship to sail us across the Mediterranean to Famagusta in Cyprus.

Trucks were laid on to take us into the capital Nicosia where we were staying in a NAAFI hostel. As soon as we arrived, a note was given to me telling me to report to the Military Police Headquarters which was only a couple of blocks away. I told the Sergeant who I was and he said that he understood I had had my kit stolen on the train. He said he had arranged for me to collect some more kit from the Royal Welsh Fusiliers who were camped about two miles outside the town. He gave me directions and I set off.

I found the camp and a Lieutenant in the quartermaster's store. He let me have a shirt, vest, underpants, socks, a towel and another pack just to tide me over whilst I was on leave. I should have had them in pairs but I would have to get the rest when I got back to Tel El Kebir. I made the best of my leave but this incident spoiled it, knowing that when I got back there I would be on a charge for losing army property.

When our leave was over, we got the boat again from Famagusta to Haifa, then the train back through Palestine to Tel El Kebir without any further problems. The following day I had to report to the Company Sergeant Major who told me I was on a charge for losing army property. Of course, with it all having been reported to the Military Police the evidence had to come from GHQ Cairo back to our place before I could be tried and sentenced. This all took time and I was due to go on demob, and anyone facing a charge of any sort was not allowed to go on demob until it was all cleared up, so I was kept back for a couple of weeks until my hearing.

I was then marched in by the Company Sergeant Major in front of the Commanding Company Officer, whose name was Colonel Norris. He was a real gentleman. The charge was read out by the Sergeant Major with another Corporal as witness. I remember I had to swear on *The Bible* to tell the truth, but the other Corporal wouldn't as he was an agnostic, in other words he had no belief so he had to swear on some other oath. The Colonel then asked me how I pleaded and asked me if I had anything to say. The answer was 'No Sir, I'm guilty.'

He then said, 'Consider I have given you a reprimand and that is the end of the matter.' Then he said to me, 'I understand you are still short of kit.' I replied that I was. He then said, 'My staff car is outside and I work in the quartermaster's store so I will run you up there and get you fitted up.' We both got into the back seat, of course he had a driver and a high ranking officer like a Colonel or above always flew a flag on the bonnet and any troops walking about had to salute. It was quite an experience. There I was having just been on a charge and I was now sitting in the Colonel's car and everyone was saluting us as we went along.

We got to the stores and the Colonel went in and got the kit I was short of. He came out and said that he would run me back to camp. So off we went with more salutes. We got back to camp and Colonel Norris got out with me and said, 'You will be on your way to the UK for demob in a few days Corporal so I won't see you any more.' He shook hands with me and wished me all the best back home. I thought, *what a nice way to end my service overseas!*

**Billy Banks Royal Corp of Signals, Joiner Frae Freckleton.
Egypt 1946**

Chapter 11
Demob

Within a couple of days I was on the train with all my kit leaving Tel El Kebir for the last time. I had to go to the port of Alexandria and into another transit camp to wait for a ship. Things were very lax in the camp, we had no duties of any sort - there was just roll call each morning then we went swimming in the Mediterranean.

The second morning on parade we were all given a slip of paper to write down our names, home address and nearest railway station. I bent down to write on my knee and the chap next to me must have been watching me write and he gave me a nudge. I looked up and he said, 'I know thee.' I then stood up to look at him but couldn't put a name to his face and I said that I couldn't remember him. He then said in a broad Lancashire accent, 'Tha knows me.'

'No,' I said, 'I can't place you.'

He said, 'Tha knows Billy Banks, joiner, frae Freckleton.'

I looked, and couldn't believe my eyes, 'Aye Billy,' I said, laughing, 'I never expected seeing you stood beside me.'

He then asked how long had I been out there and I said I'd been there for over three and a half years.

'How long?' he said.

I replied, 'Over three and a half years.'

He then said, 'I thought I'd bin out here a long time, I've been in Cairo twelve months.'

I said, 'Billy, you are talking to an old campaigner now.' We had quite a laugh.'

'Ar ta going on demob?' he said.

I replied, 'I am.'

He then said, 'We can go home together.'

'Yes we can,' I said. However, as I was hoping to visit Trixie in Sussex I knew I would have to tell him about this at some time during the journey.

A few days later we embarked on the troopship called *Empire Battleaxe*. It was quite a modern ship with bunk beds for sleeping. We left port, sailed down the Med past Malta again, past Sicily then up past Sardinia, past Corsica and eventually docked in Toulon in the South of France. During our sail down the Mediterranean we overtook two British submarines and our ship signalled them to ask them to dive for us; they did so and it was a splendid sight. Then they radioed us to say they had us in their periscope sights

Trooper Empire Battleaxe - Alexander Egypt to Toulon France.
1946

ready to sink us, however, as we were a friendly ship they would turn a blind eye. They were also going to Portsmouth to be decommissioned, demob and home. When they resurfaced they were well behind us but it was a sight to remember.

We went into a transit camp at Toulon for about four days to await a train to take us to Calais in Northern France, which took two days and nights on the train. At Calais we got straight onto the cross channel ferry and soon saw the *"White Cliffs of Dover"* that Vera Lynn sang about. Then there was a train waiting to take us to Guildford and we had one night there.

The following morning we had breakfast as soldiers for the last time and it was then that I told Billy Banks that I was going to see someone down in Sussex, and Billy was on to it like a shot:

'Thar going to see a woman art a?'

'That's right,' I said.

'Tha doesn't need to bother,' he said, 'I'll say nowt;' and I don't think Billy ever did.

After breakfast we handed in our kit except for what we stood up in. We then had to choose suits, shirts, socks, ties, shoes, caps, trilbies, bowler hats etc., and we were civilians once more after five and a half years as soldiers. Everything was packed into a cardboard box. Billy went on his way back home, while I travelled by train to Brighton. I remember it was Friday, August Bank Holiday weekend.

When I arrived at Brighton it would have been about 2pm, I put my cardboard box with civilian clothes into the left luggage office then went to the telephone. I had never used a telephone before and I remember Trixie had told me in a letter that the phone number was 28. I felt rather nervous about it and asked if it was Trixie's mother. She said it was so I said, 'We haven't met and you don't know me but I have been writing to Trixie for a few weeks from Egypt.'

'Oh,' she said, 'you must be Syl.'

'That's right,' I said, 'I am in Brighton and I wonder if Trixie will meet me here somewhere?'

She said that Trixie wasn't home from work and said she thought it would be better if I went to Henfield. She told me where the bus station was in Brighton and I wended my way down there. As it was the Bank Holiday weekend there were huge queues for buses so I joined the queue for Henfield. The bus came in, filled up, another bus came in, filled up, and I was still in the queue. I managed to get on the third bus. We set off through the lovely Sussex South Downs and after we had been going awhile I asked the conductor if he knew where West End Lane was, but he didn't. However, there was a Corporal sat on a seat who overheard our conversation and he turned to me and said he knew where West End Lane was, he lived in Henfield. When the bus stopped in the village it was a place about as big as Freckleton with the main road running through. We both got off and the Corporal gave me directions to my destination and said I would see a church down there. He went off in the opposite direction and off I went on a beautiful sunny afternoon.

I hadn't gone far when I saw a girl in a lovely summer dress sitting on her bike on the other side of the road. I thought she looked like Trixie from the photograph I had. She came riding across to me and said, 'You must be Syl.'

'That's right,' I said. And that's how we met.

So we went walking along, me pushing the bike which was like new. We turned down West End Lane past the church to her home, a little semi-detached cottage just over the railway bridge near Henfield railway station. Life seemed all roses on that beautiful Friday afternoon. She introduced me to her mother, a lovely lady, and her father, who wasn't very well. Sadly, unknown to me he was dying. I remember that her mother made me a salad tea. We all talked for a while and they asked me about their son Maurice, who would be demobbed a couple of weeks later.

Trixie took me for a walk down to the river and when we came back her mother asked me to stay the night, then I could set off for home the following day, but I declined. I have often regretted that because they were very nice to me. At 8pm Trixie came down to the station with me, the train came, I kissed her goodbye and gave her some scent I had bought in Toulon.

I arrived in Brighton about 9pm to catch a train to London, I think the station was Victoria. I got there about 10pm, then had to get to Euston Station. I went down the escalator to the underground platform, I had never been on the tube train before and I watched several trains come and go. I then went to a man on the platform to ask which trains went to Euston as I hadn't travelled on the tube before. He told me that all the trains were going to Euston and he said that when we got on the train he would tell me how to read the route shown on the roof, so I learned quite a lot on that demob day. I got to Euston about 10.45pm and my train for

Preston was at 11 o'clock. I arrived there at about 5am and caught the 6am bus to Freckleton and home.

As I look back I was one of the lucky ones to go through five and a half years in the army, travel thousands and thousands of miles and to come home unscathed. Not so for many. I remembered back to June 1939 when I and another apprentice at HV Burlingham Caravans had to register for military service. His name was Arthur Kavanagh and he lived in Inkerman Street in Ashton, just off Blackpool Road at the foot of the big railway bridge. His mother had a grocer's and confectioner's shop. When we got stopped at HV Burlingham's because the government commandeered all the material for war work Arthur brought my tool box home for me in his father's little Ford car one Saturday afternoon in September. I remember it was a bright sunny afternoon as we sat on the front garden wall before he went back to Ashton. He asked me what I was going to do. I said that I was going to make myself a new toolbox.

I have never forgotten his reply which was, 'You are being a bit optimistic considering we have a war in front of us.'

I answered, 'Well, we have to look on the bright side Arthur.'

I have often thought he must have had a premonition because I never saw him again. We had both registered at the same time for military service. We both went for a medical to Pole Street in Preston the same week, and it was there where they told us which regiment we had to go in. I was for the Royal Army Ordnance Corps, and later when the Royal Electrical Mechanical Engineers was formed I was transferred to them. Arthur had to go into the Royal Army Service Corps as he had a driving licence. I suppose they must have needed drivers because Arthur was called up in October 1939 and had a month's infantry training. He was then shipped over to France before Christmas. He was stationed on the French Belgium border all winter, but when the Germans began their offensive in May 1940, marching through Holland and Belgium, blitzing the border with bombs, Arthur's company were told to get out of their billets and retreat. Arthur got out with the rest then told his mate that he had forgotten something. He went back into the billet which then got a direct hit with a bomb, and sadly nothing was ever found of Arthur, he was "missing, believed killed in action". Such a sad end to a 20 year old lad. That was about nine months after we had shaken hands wishing each other the best of luck. How lucky I was.

No doubt many people reading this in years to come will wonder what became of Trixie. After I had visited her in 1946 her brother Maurice got demobbed and came back home. Not long after that their father died, then Maurice got married and went to live in Shoreham in Sussex. Trixie and her mother lived together in Henfield and Trixie went to work as a telephonist. Sussex was a long way from Lancashire and we didn't have much money in those days. We wrote to each other occasionally which dwindled down to a letter and Christmas card each Christmas until she died. Her mother wrote to tell me that Trixie was being given a ride home from work with a young man in his car on 4th January 1968 when she was taken ill in his car and was taken to hospital. It seems she had a stroke and sadly died in hospital the next day, aged 46. She had never married and I was very sad to hear this news; I decided to go to her funeral.

I left Preston by train in early January to go to Brighton, where I stayed the night. Next morning I caught the bus to Henfield, the same route I had taken when I first went to see Trixie. I got off the bus at the same bus stop and started to walk down the main street where I had first met her on that beautiful sunny afternoon in August 1946. My mind travelled back to seeing her sitting on her bike across the road in her lovely summer dress, much different to this January morning with all the fields covered in snow. I came to West End Lane feeling very sad as I walked past the village church where the funeral was to take place. Her mother and Maurice were very surprised to see me but made me very welcome. I felt very sorry for her mother who would now be alone.

After the funeral had taken place we went back to the house for a drink and then I had to leave to get the bus to Brighton. Maurice came with me to the bus stop and I was on my way back home feeling very sad. After that Trixie's mother lived alone until she died in her early eighties. She and I always kept in touch at Christmas with a card and letter until she died. She was a lovely woman, so was Trixie. She was 25, two years younger than me when I first met her. Since her mother died Maurice and I still keep in touch at Christmas. It is now 2002 so I have known him a long time. So that is the story about what happened to Trixie, a nice friend. I have memories of very happy times and sad ones too, but that is life.

As regards the Scotsman, Joe Lickerish, whom I had been friendly with whilst stationed at Bonhill in Scotland, I wrote to him from Iraq and it was about four months before I got a reply. It seemed not long after I was drafted, Joe was put on a draft and my letter to Bonhill in Scotland caught up with him in Mombassa in East Africa. He wrote to me in Iraq saying he had at last got my letter and the envelope was covered in addresses back and front until it finally found him. I wrote back to Mombassa but never got a reply so lost track of him.

However, forty three years after being put on overseas draft from Bonhill, I and my late wife Dolly, were on holiday in Scotland staying in Oban. On one particular day we went to a restaurant, which was also the Oban Concert Hall, and just in the entrance were three telephone booths with telephone books for different areas. I said to Dolly that I would see if I could find a number for Joe Lickerish. I looked in the Stirling area directory but there wasn't one Lickerish, so I then looked in the Lomond directory, which covered the Bonhill district and where Joe had married Betty McPhearson, a local girl. Sure enough there were three people listed in the name of Lickerish, two with the initial J.

I rang a number and a woman answered. I asked if she was Mrs Lickerish and she replied that she was. I then asked if her husband's name was Joe and she said that it was. I asked her if he had been stationed at Bonhill Camp REME in 1941-42 and she said that he had been. I then told her that I knew him and that I had also been stationed at Bonhill and that my name was Till. I could hear her asking her husband if he knew someone at Bonhill Camp called Till and I could hear him answer that he never knew anyone called Till. She then came back on the telephone and said that Joe had never known anyone called Till, so I said that my first name was Sylvester, so she told her husband this. Immediately I could hear Joe say that he did know me, and he came to the phone and asked me where I was. I told him that Dolly and I were at Oban but we were on our way home the following day via Loch Lomond. He asked us to call and see him, so we arranged to meet the following day at about 1 o'clock on Balloch car park.

We met up the following day and Joe took us to his home in Balloch. Word had got around about this meeting and there were newspaper men there and photographers. It was quite a reunion and we had a lovely time. We met Betty, his wife, and his two daughters, Karen and Elizabeth. That was in 1985.

Sadly my wife Dolly died in 1988 and Joe died about two or three years later. They did come to stay with us for a week before Dolly died, but since then Betty, Karen and Elizabeth phone me nearly every month to ask if I am alright, which is very kind of them.

So that is my story. It may make interesting reading for someone in a few years time.

I swear before God that all I have written in this story is absolutely true.

Sylvester Till
May 26th 2002

Appendix
I

Memories and Data of *Britannic III*

She was built in 1930 by Harland and Wolf, Belfast, as a passenger liner for Cunard White Star Line, to carry 1,000 passengers. She was the largest ship afloat at that time.

She weighed 27,000 tons and had eight decks. She was converted into a troopship in 1939 and carried troops for Sicily landings (Operation Husky). By the end of the war she had carried 180,000 troops and steamed 376,000 miles.

7,000 of us embarked on her from Hunter's Quay, Dunoon, Firth of Clyde, Scotland, when we sailed to pick up a convoy on about 18th December 1942 on our way to Durban, via Freetown, West Africa. We had to zigzag a great deal in the Atlantic Ocean to avoid U-boats, and many of us suffered severe seasickness. Whereas we had a Royal Navy escorting convoy we only ever saw one frigate, which came through the convoy to wish us all a Merry Christmas over her megaphone.

At a guess I would think there were about 8 or 10 ships in the convoy, cargo boats, tankers and troopships. The *Britannic* was the flagship. The troopship ahead of us was the *Caernarfon Castle,* and behind us was the *Orion.*

On that voyage our ship's foghorn was blowing all night most nights if any U-boats were about. One blast told the whole convoy to zigzag to port for about fifteen minutes, and two blasts meant zigzag to starboard. Even though there were no lights shown, it was amazing how the ships had kept quite good position in the dark.

We stood off Freetown on 1st January 1943 to refuel and take on fresh water.

We docked in Durban about the middle of January, then went into a transit camp for a month whilst waiting for another ship.

In 1947 she reverted back to a Cunard passenger liner and in winter cruised from New York to the Caribbean and in summer from Liverpool to New York in summer.

Her final sailing was on 16th December 1961 under her own power from Liverpool to Thomas Ward, Inverkithing in Scotland, to be broken up as scrap. What a sad end to such a wonderful ship.

The ship's bell of the Britannic is now on display in the Marine Museum at Albert Dock, Liverpool.

Britannic III Ship's Bell, now in the Maritime Museum at Royal Albert Dock, Liverpool.

Appendix
II

Details of *Felix Roussel*

Troopship *Felix Roussel,* a French passenger liner in peacetime, and lying in port during World War II.

She appeared to be flying the French flag.

She was taken over by the Ministry of War Transport (Bibby Bros & Co. Managers).

This ship took us from Durban in February 1943 up the Indian Ocean to Bombay in India, standing off Mombassa, East Africa, to disembark some troops, before proceeding to Bombay docks where we just transferred to another French troopship, the *Cap St Jacques.*

It took two weeks to sail from Durban to Bombay, zigzagging up the Indian Ocean to avoid U-boats.

Appendix
III

Details of *Cap St Jacques*

This is *Cap St Jacques* was under way during World War II. It was a French cargo ship, which had been turned into a troopship, and we were accommodated on her in the ship's holds.

It was taken over by the Ministry of War Transport in 1941 and sailed under the British flag. This ship took us from Bombay at about the end of February, sailing further up the Indian Ocean and the Arabian Sea through the Straits of Hormuz into the Persian Gulf, right to the northern end of the Gulf into the Shatt Al Arab waterway, to disembark at Al Basra in Iraq. We were then taken out to the Sheiba desert, which was about ninety miles away.

The journey from Bombay to Al Basra took about two weeks, so we arrived there about the middle of March 1943. So you can see that we did quite a bit of sailing from the 18th December 1942 when we left Scotland!